TOYS, PLAY AND DISCIPLINE
IN CHILDHOOD

TOYS, PLAY AND DISCIPLINE
IN CHILDHOOD

by

BEATRIX TUDOR-HART
Formerly Principal, Fortis Green School

LONDON
ROUTLEDGE AND KEGAN PAUL

First published in 1955
by Routledge and Kegan Paul Ltd.
Broadway House · 68-74 Carter Lane,
London, E.C.4.
Reprinted 1970
Reproduced and Printed in Great Britain by
Redwood Press Limited,
Trowbridge & London

ISBN 0 7100 6871 9 (c)
ISBN 0 7100 6872 7 (p)

To
MY DAUGHTER
WHO TAUGHT ME MUCH

Contents

INTRODUCTION

CHAPTER I. BABYHOOD
(0–2 *years*)

CHAPTER II. THE NURSERY YEARS
(2–6 *years*)

Contents

CHAPTER III. THE DISCIPLINE OF THE NURSERY YEARS

CHAPTER IV. THE SOCIAL LIFE OF THE NURSERY

Contents

CHAPTER V.   A NURSERY SCHOOL DAY

CHAPTER VI.   THE SCHOOL CHILD

CHAPTER VII.   THE DISCIPLINE OF LATER CHILDHOOD

CHAPTER VIII.   THE SCHOOL CHILD'S SOCIAL LIFE

Contents

CHAPTER IX.   THE PRIMARY SCHOOL'S TASK

Illustrations

Introduction

DURING twenty-five years of teaching children between the ages of two and twelve years I have come to realize how closely linked play and discipline are in the development of young children. I have learnt this by experience, not through theory, for there are no books which deal with this connection. There are few books which deal with play, and my experience has led me to the conclusion that many parents need advice and welcome help in catering for their childrens' needs. During the second world war we had to open hundreds of day nurseries, at short notice, to cater for children whose mothers were required for war work. This need found us quite unprepared. There was a deplorable lack of women trained to know and understand the needs of young children of pre-school age. This lack of understanding showed itself most in the kind of play material, or very often just in the absence of play material, which was provided for the children—particularly the smaller ones—those between one and two years of age. It also showed itself, however, in the way in which the behaviour of the children was handled. Among those who answered the appeal for nursery helpers were many ex-teachers, and these were often the persons who least knew how to manage the children. This was not because they

Introduction

were bad teachers but because their training and experience had been for the classroom. The classroom, even for five-year-olds, before the last war, took the child out of his normal living context and placed him in a relatively artificial one, in which the world of play and its social discipline was unknown. What opportunity has the average teacher of watching children at play or of taking part in their activities?

Since 1940 some infant schools, but by no means all, have improved in the provision of play material, but most are still so overcrowded and underequipped that it is not easy to provide as much play with its play discipline as children really require.

It is important not only to know why and how children require to play, but to understand the kind of play material which they need at different ages for their various kinds of play.

The chief purpose of play material is to forward the child's development, physical, mental and emotional; suitable toys and play equipment will help, bad ones will hinder it. It is not only toys made or bought by the adults which will help the small child to develop successfully; it is probable he learns more and gains more satisfaction from the material he provides himself with if he is given reasonable opportunity; for instance, earth, stones, sticks, water, sand and, in fact, all he finds in the garden and out of doors generally, and the odds and ends he succeeds in picking up indoors, empty cotton-reels, bits of string, old cartons and flour bags, as well as old kitchen utensils his mother discards; all these objects of everday life should be at a child's disposal at home; they are usually there for the having. At a nursery school they may have to be deliberately collected by the staff, and should be.

Play material is needed for the child to learn to know his

own world, the objects which are presented to him by his five senses. He also needs toys to learn, train and practice his newly found skills, e.g., grasping, holding, throwing, walking and climbing; co-ordination of hand, eye and brain, such as building; he needs to stimulate his imagination, through which he satisfies so many emotional needs and feelings.

The older child needs play equipment both to practice skills and to satisfy imagination and creative energy just as much as the child of nursery age.

GOOD AND BAD PLAY MATERIAL

Play material can be divided into five chief categories:

(*a*) That which helps the child to experiment with and discover the nature of the world around him. For this he needs to be allowed to explore and to handle as far as possible all the objects in his environment. The most important of these are water, sand, earth, clay and paints.

(*b*) That which stimulates creative activity, initiative and effort, sand, clay, paints, chalks.

(*c*) That which stimulates the imagination—dolls, dressing-up clothes, farmyard animals.

(*d*) That which helps the child to attain adult skill, e.g., brushes and brooms, scissors to cut with.

(*e*) That which directly helps the development of physical and mental abilities, e.g., gymnastic apparatus, constructional toys.

Mechanical toys which can be put to no useful purpose but which can only be wound up to go, serve only to stimulate a desire for novelty and breed boredom and restlessness. They are easily broken, and this leads to carelessness and destruction. Good toys given at the wrong time and at the wrong stage are as harmful as bad toys.

Introduction

A very sound principle is to make as much use as possible of simple objects of everyday life. Sticks, stones, old cotton-reels, bits of stuff, match-sticks, etc., are often far superior for the training of imagination, initiative, and resourcefulness than elaborate toys, even those carefully planned.

Home-made toys are good. Small children like, above all things, making something; the next best is watching father or mother making it. A home-made cart, in the making of which a small child can help, satisfies two needs, and is far more highly prized than a bought one. Many toys, from a bead necklace to a doll, can be made at home, and I would recommend them above others.

It is never desirable to buy elaborate toys nor expensive ones, except when buying big things such as carts, trucks, trains, wheelbarrows, etc. It is better to buy one big, solid cart, or a really well-made but not too big train, than several small and fragile ones.

For small children, anyone clever with a fretsaw can make home-made fitting toys out of wood. Building blocks are worth spending money on; they will be used for years, and the large hollow ones are far superior to small solid ones, if they are available.

Solidly, well-built play-material can always be passed on when one child has outgrown it, and a friend's babies are sure to welcome it gladly.

Since independence, initiative, and self-reliance are characteristics we should aim at developing in our children it is natural that one of the qualities of good material should be that it stimulates and encourages these traits. That is to say, material which a small child can use, understand and enjoy on his own, with which he can make and create things entirely unaided, is better than material which necessitates the help of a grown-up.

4

Introduction

WHAT NEEDS DO TOYS SATISFY?

A child's greatest ambition is to be grown-up and to do what the grown-ups do. A baby naturally wants to clean, sweep, scrub, wash, iron, carry things about, open and shut doors, and do all the other hundred-and-one things the men and womenfolk do about the house and garden. Far from being prevented from doing these things he should be encouraged and helped. The help we can give is in providing him with tools which are suitable to his size for these activities.

The popularizing of psychological knowledge has helped to bring on to the market a flood of 'educational' toys, many of which are very good and suitable, but many of which, also, while purporting to satisfy certain 'psychological' needs and 'instinctive urges' of the child, are not of much value; for they involve activities which the child does not in practice undertake for their own sake but for the sake of obtaining an ulterior end. A good example of this sort of unsuitable educational toy is the lacing, buttoning or other frames of the Montessori equipment. A child does not want to amuse himself buttoning; he wants to be able to do up his own buttons so that he can become independent. It is wise to remember that if a toy is thus a substitute for a real tool or real activity it does not fulfil a useful purpose.

Play material should always be very carefully graded to suit the child's abilities; it should always be sufficiently in advance of what he can do to stimulate intelligence and effort towards new achievements, but not so difficult that it discourages him. Children are very easily discouraged by demands which are beyond their power of achievement.

This book is written in the hope that parents and

5

teachers, who have realized that play is an important and essential part of growth and learning until childhood is left behind, will have their belief strengthened by the facts which are presented. I hope the arguments given will be sufficiently forceful to persuade those who do not know or are sceptical, and in particular teachers in the primary schools, that play, in its true sense, is as important as the 3 Rs in the first ten years of life.

DISCIPLINE

Before attempting to say how discipline shall be achieved it is essential to have a clear idea of what is understood by the word. In this book discipline is understood to be a human characteristic which has existed ever since man has been human. From the time men lived in groups, and that is, we believe, since they achieved an upright carriage, using hands as tools and speech to communicate with, they have had to have a discipline. Without discipline any community must disintegrate. It can only survive by a discipline which holds the individuals together, enabling them to work co-operatively. In any community the operative discipline will therefore depend on the structure of the social group and its conditions of living. If it were possible for a man to survive and live alone on a desert island he would have no discipline, no morals, no ethics. For these characteristics could not be developed in a single person living alone; they can only appear in the process of social living. Throughout the ages, in every civilization, a discipline has evolved, been passed on from generation to generation and gradually changed, as the social unit has changed with man's growing conquest of nature.

Discipline is then that which enables man to live with man so that all may survive and gain benefit from their

6

association. The simpler the society the simpler the discipline required to hold it together. In a primitive society, with no private property and the very simplest of communal property, the discipline will centre round organization of marriage and family, division of labour, the distribution of the product of work. This discipline is crystallized in and centralized through the initiation rites and the rituals of food production, birth, marriage and death. Because of the simplicity of their living no strict discipline need be applied to the young in a primitive society. Apart from obeying a few taboos, until their initiation into adult life at puberty, the young children are left to play as freely as they like.

Our civilization is far removed from primitive peoples. It is extremely complex, the result of thousands of years of economic and social development. But the difference between it and a primitive society which most vitally affects the rearing of children is the fact that simple people have a harmonious and homogenious social structure, a unity which is not torn by social conflict, whereas our society, particularly at the present moment, is riddled with deep cleavages. Within each nation, in the western world at least, there are the flagrant extremes of wealth and poverty, ownership and lack of possessions, class divisions which still cause much bitterness and harm. The 'wartime' conditions under which young persons who are now becoming parents have passed their own childhood, clearly show how the adult world has so far failed to solve the vital problem of peaceful existence between nations. These deep and vital problems, which must be solved if mankind is to survive, directly affect growing children. In the first place parents themselves are a prey to the conflicting social pressures which exist, and are often insecure and lacking in confidence in themselves and in their beliefs. In the second place the contrasts in our society give rise to crime, hooliganism and gangsterism. Every day anti-social trends, greed, brutality, lust for power, find spectacular expression, reported in press, radio and films. The impact of all this on young children is very great and makes the task of parents and teachers, in trying to instil high social and moral values in the children, very difficult.

Yet basically the same values are true in our civilization as they are in that of primitive peoples. If we but remember that the sole reason of discipline is the need for men to live and work harmoniously together for the benefit of all, we will understand better what we must require of young children and how we shall ask it of them. Blind obedience to the demands of adults is not likely to develop a capacity for self-discipline nor an understanding of the purpose of discipline. It is well known that anyone, and children in particular, learn anything better and quicker if they understand what it is they are learning about. It is just as true of discipline. If a child knows and understands what is being asked of him, and why, he is more likely to absorb it, remember it and, above all, be willing to accept it.

In this book I shall try to show that discipline, which, if it is to be of any service to the community must be, or become, a self discipline, can only arise in a social setting, and that in play it finds its most significant and most useful place for development.

A self discipline which grows out of daily social and practical experience is of a far slower and less spectacular kind than that of the drill hall. But those who try to apply the external discipline of fear, which is the only alternative to self-discipline, find that it affects a child's play most harmfully—in the last analysis the child may become unable to play, particularly socially. Social play sets its own high standards, which only the self-disciplined child can accept.

Introduction

We must therefore trace the impact of play on discipline and discipline on play.

There is also another discipline besides the social one. That is the discipline of reality. It is a very obvious one and, for that very reason, we tend to take it for granted and overlook its educational influence. For a small child the recognition of natural limitations, at its simplest, the fact that you must go round the table in order not to bump into a leg, is both difficult and extremely distasteful. How often do we see little children hit an object deliberately in a rage after they have just hurt themselves on it by mistake? Another facet of the same discipline is that of learning how to use tools and develop skills, manual as well as mental.

Young children must be given ample opportunity to learn this discipline, and they can only do so through practical experience. The adult world, to a very large extent, controls this experience, and can give it or withhold it, make it easier or more difficult to learn.

Chapter One

BABYHOOD

0–2 Years

THE NEED FOR PLAY

ALL young animals play and so do the human young. That is common knowledge. Yet we tend to say it and then dismiss it as one aspect of life to which we need pay little attention.

Play is not, for the young, simply relaxation from work, as it is for adults. Play is the very essence of life and the only means whereby the infant can learn anything. It remains the chief means of learning well into school years, certainly until reading has been completely mastered. It aids learning very markedly when lessons combine imaginative creative work with the facts to be learned.

It is through play that a child's physical, mental, emotional and social life grows and develops. The adults help or impede this progress by the way in which they treat the child with regard to his play, and by the kind of play material they give him. It is through play that a child gains confidence, self reliance, initiative and independence. Above all it is through play that the child makes his most important social contacts, that with his peers.

It is through and in play that the young child first learns to curb his will voluntarily, in the interest of another, to accept orders from others, to conform to group decisions, to give and take services and to share. He learns to do all these things of his own free will because in that way lies the possibility of being a recognized and well-liked member of the community. We would do well to consider what discipline and self discipline are required to reach the stage of co-operative play of four-year-olds playing an elaborate game of mother and father, hospital and doctor, captain and crew of ship or an aeroplane.

That play is very serious work is well asserted by the frequently repeated phrase 'I am too busy' when a small child is asked to leave his occupation; by the way in which younger children concentrate, sometimes for an hour at a time, on their play, sometimes even frowning, or biting their lips in their effort to get something done correctly.

THE FIRST TWO YEARS

The infant's routine

From the moment he is born a baby is a social being, even though he has no self consciousness and no knowledge of other beings. He cannot survive without the constant care of at least one adult. His whole development takes place within a social framework. Almost everything that happens to him occurs through the activity of human beings. All his needs are met by human beings (or not met!) and life appears to his growing mind either good or bad according to whether his needs have been well, or badly, met.

A baby's needs are, relative to an older child's, fairly simple. Yet, simple as they are, it is remarkable how many mothers and nurses fail to meet them, largely because of faulty teaching, or ignorance. Self-consciousness, that is the ability to be conscious of yourself as a separate person, distinct from other separate persons, begins to show itself somewhere between eighteen months and two years. Since discipline has no real meaning apart from self-discipline for social purposes, the training of a small baby to do 'as he is told' is obviously useless. A baby does not 'do as he is told'. He does as his needs drive him. His basic needs are for food, warmth, the elimination of pain when it appears, sleep, the exercise of his five senses and social contact. These are all real needs, which require to be met if the baby is to grow into a healthy, contented and intelligent child. Since an infant does not understand his relationship with the human world, he only expresses his needs when he feels them. He does not invent them in order to 'get the attention' of mother or nurse as so many people seem to think. When he wants something he cries for it, for that is the only means at his disposal during the first two years of life. Although there has been, in recent years a certain retreat among some members of the medical and nursing professions from the strict 'habit-training' which came into vogue with the Truby King methods of infant feeding and care, there is still a widespread acceptance of the idea that babies can be 'trained' into certain routines of eating, sleeping and playing. If, by a miracle, the routine adopted happens to suit the particular needs of the baby concerned, all goes well. But all babies differ as much in the quantity of food, sleep, clothing, etc., which they require, as they do in the physical characteristics which they inherit. So every baby has to establish his own rhythm of feeding, sleeping and waking, and mothers and nurses must accept it, if they wish the children to grow strong and healthy.

The daily routine of the baby is the earliest form of discipline, but one which the baby imposes on the adult world and which changes both as the baby grows and changes, and as circumstances in his environment change.

Babyhood

There is nothing ever static in life. The baby makes his needs felt and changes the environment. The environmental changes, in their turn, affect the baby. The simplest example of this interchange is the baby's cry for food, the giving of food and the baby's satisfied feeding.

If an infant's own rhythm of feeding, eating and sleeping is not accepted it affects not only his physical health but it affects very considerably his ability to develop mentally. In practice this means he is unable to devote energy and attention to play. The unhappy infant that cries for long periods at a time, that is a bad and restless sleeper, will not develop his abilities to crawl, walk, climb, to use his hands and to co-ordinate hand and eye movements as well as the contented baby who sleeps well and is healthy. We have known for some time now that older children who are seriously disturbed mentally are nearly always seriously retarded in many ways, particularly of course, academically. It is equally true of babies. But naturally with them the disturbance is not so severe, the retardation not so great as with older children.

The baby's first four needs soon cease to be his only ones. By the end of the first month a child begins to respond to the attention of mother or nurse. Before his feeds and at bath and washtime his crying can be stilled by nursing and singing. When he is awake he will respond to play and soon be smiling and laughing his appreciation. His playtime with mother is a real need for the small baby and will remain so for many years. Playing with a small child at bathtimes and often during his waking hours is part of that intimate companionship and love which should exist between mother and child if both are to be happy. The baby needs this kind of attention more frequently than the older child, if he is to develop well. It gives greater stimulus to his own activities in search of knowledge.

Babyhood

Where there are older children in the family this stimulus to activity, which is the fun of being played with, is much richer for the small child, for he has several persons to entertain him instead of one. His mother can free herself for other work when one of the older children will play with baby.

As he grows older his waking periods become longer and often by five or six months he is no longer willing to be laid in a pram out of earshot or sight, as soon as he has been fed. Even if he will still go to sleep later on, his awareness of the world, particularly of his mother, makes him demand companionship. He will want to be either where he can see and hear her or where he can see and hear other children or adults. To give in to his demands is not to spoil him and be lacking in disciplinary courage, but to recognize the growth of his understanding and welcome his progress. If his need for companionship is met in this way he will sleep more soundly during his rest hours and he will play by himself more contentedly for short periods of time. As the baby grows older his need for sleep lessens. By four or five months he is no longer falling asleep as he finishes his evening feed, as he used to do. It is not surprising, therefore, that he may well begin to protest at bedtime, as well as during the daytime. At whatever age this protest appears, it is useless to ignore it, for we only lay up greater trouble for ourselves by doing so. The trouble may take the form of disturbed nights, nightmares, screaming every time he is put down or left, and even going off his food and becoming ill. It is not only at a new stage of development that a baby may suddenly object to being put to bed. A change of home, or a visit, which necessitates sleeping in a strange room, is enough to bring about this change. If the child is comforted and nursed to sleep—he may, of course, only require his mother

14

to stay in the room with him—he may soon readjust himself, regain his old willingness to be put down in his cot. He may, on the other hand, be requiring to have his sleep time shortened by postponing bedtime for half an hour or so. Whatever the cause of the baby's refusal to be put down to sleep, it must be accepted. He will only sleep soundly if he goes to sleep happy and comforted. A baby that has to cry himself to sleep will become a very difficult and miserable child.

First sensations

As soon as the baby is born he embarks on his long journey of discovery which will, in fact, continue as long as he lives. But in his first two years he will learn more and make more progress than in any other four years of his life. From being unable to do anything but suck he will grow into a small child who can walk, run, climb, feed himself, put on and take off some of his clothes, understand speech, talk a little himself and play with almost any toy, from a doll to a building brick and truck. That is, he will do all this if the adults give him the opportunity to do so.

For the first two or three months the baby sleeps most of the day and wakes only to feed and sleep again. He has not much time to exercise any of his faculties. Yet from birth the need to absorb food has given his mouth a great sensitivity centred round his sucking reflex. There is little doubt that the satisfaction and comfort of receiving food, combined with the warmth and security of being nursed helps to build up the intense pleasure which he takes in sucking. This act is the one which brings the first dim understanding of something of the world outside his own body. He comes to recognize that the nipple of his mother's breast or the teat of his bottle is that which will provide his mouth with the delightful milk he wants so much. His first lesson about the world! His mouth will remain his most sensitive touchstone for testing whether anything is pleasant or nasty for several years. At first he can only suck when he is given the breast or bottle by his mother. The pleasure and satisfaction which sucking food have brought are reawakened to some degree by the sensation of sucking his fist, thumb or fingers. It is fairly certain that this pleasure helps the baby to learn through practice to control his hands until, long before he can grasp, hold and bring objects to his mouth, he is able to bring his hand up deliberately and then lie triumphantly and contentedly sucking it. If the adult world tries to interfere with the infant's activity by forcefully stopping this activity, as for instance by tying down the baby's hands, or putting bitter aloes on the fingers, far more harm will be done mentally and emotionally than will ever be done to finger or mouth by sucking.

Once a child has begun to feel his hands and feet and to realize how he can use them, his demands begin to increase rapidly. All his five senses begin to develop and we must cater for this development.

Sense training

It begins, in fact, the moment a baby can seize and hold an object; this varies with different children, but the average age is four months. From then onwards a child rapidly learns to co-ordinate hand and eye movements, to focus and to grasp. He has to learn to judge distance, size, and shape; colour comes later, well after two. He must also learn to distinguish sounds; sound sensations are keenly appreciated by very young babies. It is interesting to note how early a young baby appreciates the difference between the human voice on the one hand and all other sounds on the other. He not only differentiates between the two kinds as early as the end of the second month (many babies even before that), but the difference in his behaviour is very significant; when he hears a voice he shows immediate and obvious pleasure and expectancy; if the person does not appear soon after the voice has been heard the baby begins to cry. When he hears any other kind of noise he is usually attentive for a few seconds and then, if the sound is not repeated, his attention wanders off to something else, but he is not disappointed and unhappy as he is when a person fails to appear when he has heard a voice. This is a clear indication of the important emotional part human beings play in a baby's life.

From six months till the close of the second year it must not be forgotten that children are teething, and that, further, the sense of taste is the only sense which has yet been developed, and consequently the only one by which a baby can 'judge' an object to his own satisfaction.

In planning suitable toys for this age these two things must be kept in mind. Everything must be suitable for sucking. Everything must be calculated to help the child develop his sense of distance, shape, size and sound. He develops these senses through his interest in the objects around him.

A baby will try to seize everything within reach. My own daughter at about four months began to notice the face flannel with which she was washed. She was fascinated by it and followed its every movement; when it disappeared, she wriggled and pulled herself to the edge of the rubber bath and looked over it; then she began to cry, and was only pacified when the flannel reappeared. The next day a rubber doll was given to her and her attention was absorbed for weeks. In this way, if we are on the look-out for such signs, a child will often show us what are his needs.

Wooden toys are always best; they are washable—they

can be sucked with safety. Colour and sound-producing toys are important, but grading of either is beyond the child's capacities.

Toys should always be sufficiently small to be easily grasped and held by the small hand, but not so small that they are difficult to see or grasp or easy to swallow.

The simpler the shapes used the better. Strings of large round or square beads, small balls, square and oblong blocks are best.

For sounds, hollow bowls or boxes filled with rattling beads or pebbles are excellent. Common household objects such as empty cotton-reels, spoons, etc., are just as good as beads and pegs and blocks which are bought.

It is wise to have a pen to put a baby in, for then he can be safely left alone with his toys to amuse himself; but this should only be at times when mother is busy doing other things and cannot attend to him. He will learn to be independent and to occupy himself, and this is the basis of future self-reliance and initiative. He will, however, only be willing to be left alone for short periods of time; from the time he is able to sit alone and begin moving himself about a little, the younger the child the less time he will tolerate being alone; and a wise mother, while encouraging independent play will not enforce isolation on her baby when he asks for companionship. If she is very busy for a long time at a stretch she will peep at the child from time to time, talk to him and even play a few seconds at peek-a-boo. This occasional contact helps to keep a baby safe and secure in his mother's love.

With many children it is already possible, and therefore desirable, to begin grading material for sense training as early as fifteen or sixteen months. They are certainly sufficiently skilled and intelligent to begin constructive efforts such as placing blocks on top of each other, fitting

easy objects into their correct places. Between sixteen
months and two years, these should be of the simplest kind,
and very wide grading, if any. The Montessori and other
fitting toys which can now be obtained from the several
good toy shops listed at the back of the book, are all
suitable.

From sixteen months or so onwards till well into the
third year 'fitting' toys—wooden ones are always best—
are some of the best material which can be used: similarly
material for colour grading is good.

Social play

It is natural for mothers to play with their babies; they
play with them for their own delight long before the babies
actively respond; it is part of that good mothering small
children need. Very soon baby is responding to such games
as 'this is the way the lady rides' and 'this little pig went
to market' when his toes are being dried after the bath.
All mothers know only too well what a delightful game it
is to throw your toys out of the pram or pen in order that
Mummy shall pick them up and return them to you; the
baby never tires of that game, nor of playing peek-a-boo
behind hands or the pram-hood; a baby that gets a suffici-
ency of attention of this kind will willingly spend part of
his waking time alone, happily busying himself with his
own discoveries; for he is confident of his mother's love
and her readiness to attend to his requirements.

Conversely a baby that is trained to be left alone a
considerable part of his waking time, because it is thought
to teach him independence, will, in time, if more is expected
of him than he can tolerate, break down and refuse to be
left alone at all, and he will begin to cry the moment he
feels he is about to be set down on the floor or put in his
pram or cot. It is as if his normal confidence in the adults

had disappeared and with this confidence often also goes his ability and willingness to occupy himself and hence his capacity to learn.

From the earliest age music evokes instinctive response in a child. From the time he was born his mother has sung to him; to be crooned, or sung to, is one of his birthrights, and one he should not be deprived of; it is but another aspect of this good relationship with his mother, and he quickly learns to respond with great delight; long before he can sing himself he responds with rythmic movements and crowing. At first it is his mother's singing he likes best, but soon he will take pleasure in the music-makers, and the old-fashioned musical boxes cannot be improved upon for giving delight to a baby.

Early discipline

In the first year of life the infant does not so much play as prepare himself for play. He does this by daily practice in the development of his senses. He must learn to see, hear, taste, feel and smell. He must also practice his vocal chords and by dint of frequent exercise prepare them for the intricate details of articulation which he will later on require for speech. He must exercise his limbs so that he may walk and his hands that he may learn to use them to some purpose. This activity can only take place effectively in a happy and contented baby.

How intimately discipline is linked with activity. Treatment of the child which leads to constant or continuous crying hampers it all.

It is not only in his needs for food, sleep and companionship that the baby requires sympathetic understanding. From the time he learns to move about, anywhere from the sixth to the twelfth month, he is liable to become a danger to himself and others, unless the adults are wise

I. Baby's Toy. Cotton-reels serve 101 purposes and they
can be safely sucked

IIa. Eating is often messy to be enjoyable and successful

IIb. Up the Steps. What an adventure and what fun

and farseeing. If he is treated negatively and prevented from having his natural exercise, by being strapped into a cot, a pram or a chair, for long waking periods he will not only be retarded in his development. He will either become a lethargic, uninterested baby or he will become a struggling, unhappy and aggressive one.

From the time a baby begins to crawl, the waking periods spent in a pram or chair should become progressively shorter until at about eighteen months they should have ceased altogether, except for walks. It is not easy for a harassed mother, particularly if she has other children as well as the home and husband to look after, to plan to have the time to keep an eye on a crawling or walking toddler. It is so much easier to have him safely out of harm's way in a pram or a chair! Yet here again it pays in the long run, for the reward of planning the child's day so that we are free to attend to him while he is active and moving about and do our work while he sleeps, is that we have a healthy contented child that is learning quickly. Preventing a baby from having sufficient practice in crawling and walking is not the only unsatisfactory way of dealing with the problem of moving about. It is almost as bad for the baby to be given the freedom of motion and then be stopped every few steps by an anxious mother who is afraid her darling will come to grief.

ACTIVITIES FOR THE TODDLER

Crawling and walking

As soon as a baby can crawl it is wise to use a pen only when you cannot watch him; for his most urgent impulse is to investigate the world which has now been brought within his range by his newly acquired art of walking. He will naturally feel himself imprisoned in a play-pen. A pen is very useful, however, for learning to walk, for the bars provide excellent support for the child to pull himself up by and he can walk all round still holding on, thus gaining confidence to take the plunge to balance unaided on his own two feet; but it is much more satisfactory to walk outside the pen. Crawling or walking, the child's method of investigating the world is naturally by biting, sucking, feeling and finally throwing away any and all objects which attract his attention.

This investigation of the world around him is a small child's first means of developing his growing senses and applying his intelligence to learning the nature of that world. He will reap a fuller measure of experience if his play material has accelerated his power of observation by training his sight, touch, and judgement. In his first attempts to move about, first on all-fours, then on two rather shaky legs, a child should be given independence and encouragement.

There are two major ways in which this can be done, one positive, the other negative. Both are equally important. The positive way is to provide him with material which encourages experimentation with arms and legs, a small chair and table to carry about, to climb on, and to jump from; large hollow building blocks, which are therefore light, to carry about; carts and trains to push and to pull, trucks are particularly good because they can be filled and emptied.

Old margarine boxes (well sand-papered to remove possible splinters) and cardboard cartons are just as good, particularly if they are large enough for the baby to get in and out of himself. That is a favourite occupation with children between fifteen months and two years. Babies want drawers and cupboards to open and shut and any and every kind of odds and ends as well as their own toys to put in and out of these drawers, cupboards and boxes; collecting things, distributing them, putting them in and out, fitting them, all these are absorbing occupations at this age.

The negative way is to remove as far as possible all obstacles which are beyond the child's physical ability or which are dangerous and liable to lead to an accident, thus evoking timidity and fear.

Above all a toddler should be allowed to attempt new and daring feats; bumps and falls are a necessary part of learning to negotiate the world on two feet. A child is naturally cautious. This is, I think, too often forgotten by anxious parents. Before she could walk steadily J discovered the staircase, and I was able to watch her crawl to the edge of the top step and by very careful and complicated movements cautiously turn round and feel her way down backwards; it took her nearly five minutes to negotiate the first step! But she went down the whole flight of stairs and she was only eleven months.

A child who has never been prevented from attempting adventurous feats never loses this cautiousness and learns quickly by experience what he can and cannot do.

I once took a friend's little boy, aged twenty months, for a walk on Hampstead Heath. He was fascinated by some railing which seemed made for climbing. So he climbed; it was more difficult than he had anticipated and he nearly fell through the railings on several occasions before he reached the top. The passers-by all shook their heads, but he did it, and did not fall. When he grew older he was more independent and had more initiative than most boys of his age.

Babyhood

Investigating the world

Investigating the world brings with it for the first time the possibility of getting dirty. How many mothers stop their babies from investigating the coal-bucket, the wash-basin with its fascinating taps and splashing water, the rubbish heap and the earth in the garden? Very early in the child's life we must understand the essential need for experimenting with all natural substances which are not harmful to health and life. If a child is to develop properly, not only intellectually but emotionally; if he is to gain self-confidence, assurance and independence, he must have the opportunity of making discoveries, of experimenting with all the materials he finds to hand. The most important materials of life are water, earth and sand. Handling these things involves getting dirty and we must accept this; if we plan for it in an organized manner we shall find that getting dirty is neither harmful for the child nor really very inconvenient nor distressing to the adults. When a child is playing freely indoors or out we expect him to get dirty, and clothes are carefully planned accordingly. In winter, cotton overalls, or crawlers, that are easy to wash, can be put over woolly suits or frocks; in summer cotton clothes are easily washed anyway, and when it is hot the less the child has on the better. So getting messy need present no problem.

It is absolutely essential for the baby to handle water, sand, earth; the earlier he begins the sooner he will learn how to use them sensibly, how to create and experiment with them usefully and satisfyingly. From birth a baby has experience of water, and all healthy babies love their bath-time above all else, except feeding-time perhaps. The feel of water is deeply satisfying and the adult world is well aware of how passionately fond children are of water. If we provide babies with water in a right way not only do they benefit from it but they are not a nuisance to adults. A large bowl of water in the garden, a rubber apron over the clothes, sleeves well rolled up, a stick or an old tin or enamel mug to play with, and we can safely leave him; or indoors there is no reason why a child should not occupy himself with water, either in the bathroom by the basin, or in the kitchen at the sink, when it is not being used for other purposes; if the baby has the right tools, and in this case it is a wooden spoon and/or an old mug, he will occupy himself most successfully.

Out of doors, as indoors, a crawler or toddler must test everything he finds; his surest and most natural way is his mouth, so he will put everything into his mouth, sticks, stones, earth, worms, grass, flowers. All children do that, since it is their only means of 'knowing' a thing; it is therefore our responsibility to see that they come to no harm in their investigations, not to prevent them from having this necessary experience. My own daughter had a passion for worms when she was about fifteen months old; I certainly rescued quite a number from her mouth and I am equally certain that she must have swallowed several others during the weeks that this interest lasted.

LEARNING TO BE CLEAN

Of all the things the baby has to learn in his first two years that which most frequently leads to trouble for him and for the grown-ups is bowel and bladder control. There are two reasons for this, or rather two aspects of one reason. Bowel and bladder are very closely connected with sex, and because the former also deals with waste matter to be eliminated, for the adult world these things are 'tabu' with a very marked emotional feeling round them. The social disapproval with which all matters relating to evacuation as well as to sex are dealt with, has a particularly disastrous effect on a child. He has a marked emotional feeling of pride and pleasure in his own achievements as well as being highly sensitive in those parts of his body. It is not difficult to understand this feeling. The baby's capacities are limited. He is unable to make things like his mother, such as food. The products of bowel and bladder are creations of his very own, and moreover ones he quickly learns are valued and desired by his mother. Is she not always worried when he does not produce his daily 'motion' for her? For at least the first year he is quite unaware of what is happening and why. Until a baby is about a year old the nerve tract which connects both bowel and bladder to the voluntary nervous system of the cortex is not functioning. This means in practice, that his brain receives no message when either bowel or bladder are full and must be emptied. The emptying of both is done by reflex action over which the child has no control. The deliberate control of bowel and bladder only comes gradually after the voluntary nerve tract has come into function, that is, after the age of one year. Mothers and nurses who proudly announce that they have 'trained' a baby to be clean and use a 'pot' and have had no wet or soiled diapers since the baby was four or five months old are only stating that they have succeeded in finding out the times at which both bowel and bladder function in their own particular child. Most babies evacuate at fairly regular intervals, and if a mother can save herself extra work in washing by 'catching' her baby at the right moment it is worth while, provided the baby is willing to be held out or sat on a pot for a few moments. But if the baby objects to this practice it is most unwise. The worst thing which can happen for both their sakes is that the 'pot' shall become a thing which is feared and disliked. It is better for a baby never to have seen a pot before twelve or thirteen months than to have come to hate it.

How then can a child be 'trained' to cleanliness? The answer is, of course, that he is not trained; he learns. During his second year of life the baby learns new things at a terrific speed; above all he learns to understand speech and the actions of grown-up people. He learns to stand and then to walk, and from then on he is indefatigable in trailing after the adults, watching all the time and trying to do what they do. If the grown-ups are patient, learn by observation the signs the baby gives that he is going to evacuate (all children tend to be still for some seconds before an action, and often go red in the face and grunt) and offer the pot without insistance on it, their patience will be rewarded in due course. It may take the child a few weeks, it may take him a few months; he may have setbacks when, for no clear reason, he rejects all use of a chamber and then goes back to it again! During the time he is learning to be clean, the problems concerned, the actions involved, will become incorporated in his play and his other activities. That is his way of 'learning'. A small girl developed a great love for her 'potty' during these months. It was her favourite toy and she carried it about in her arms, rather like a doll. She would frequently put it down, sit on it, get up and look intently into it, shake her head (she was not always using it at the time for its correct purpose) and pick it up again. When visitors called it was always offered as a special gift (as we might offer a home-made cake). One day she refused to have her bath— she screamed every time her mother tried to lift her up to place her in the bath. This was strange behaviour, for bath time had always been a favourite playtime. Then she suddenly ran out of the bathroom and came back carrying her pot; she stood on tiptoe trying to put the pot into the bathtub. Her mother guessed this was important to the child for some reason; for about three weeks the pot had to sit in the bathtub with her to keep her happy. This need disappeared as suddenly as it had appeared; but from then on there were very few 'accidents'.

During the months children are learning to control these bodily functions it is reasonable to expect them to show interest in, and affection for, the tools which have to be used. If the adults try to get the baby to use a pot, and at the same time say it is 'dirty' and 'don't touch', 'horrid', etc., it is confusing and bewildering for the baby who feels he is being alternately asked to and disuaded from, using it. You must be utterly consistent with young children. During the early years it is absolutely essential that children should never be given the idea that either form of evacuation is 'dirty' or 'horrid'. It should be a 'nice' thing which, done in the right place, gives pleasure and satisfaction to all concerned. As they grow older and understand more how older persons behave, children soon wish to behave as grown-ups. They begin to take a pride in being able to 'manage' alone and round about four or five are eager to close doors and tell adults to go away. We should not artificially forestall this development.

I have written about this at some length because there is still so much mishandling of this stage of development. Also because it has such a marked influence on the child's general behaviour and his ability to play. Already in the second year a child will begin to reject messy play such as water, sand, mud, paints and messy food such as custard, rice pudding, blancmange and even mashed potatoes, showing distress and horror, if too much stress has been laid on the dirtiness of puddles on the floor, or accidents in pants. Most babies show their concern with the controls they are establishing, in their play. If a mother has been in the habit of mopping up 'puddles' with the baby's help in order to strengthen the attitude that these are better not made at all, the child will be quite likely to play games of making puddles by pouring water on the floor and then mopping it up with many shakes of the head.

IMAGINATIVE PLAY

The kind of play mentioned at the end of the last section, the reproduction of acts carried out by adults, appears during the second year, mostly during the second half of this year, because speech and the significance of adults actions is being sufficiently understood.

The first signs of real speech begin at about a year; by eighteen months a baby has a sufficient vocabulary to express his feelings and wants, and it is at about this age that imaginative play begins. It makes its first appearance usually with dolls; this play material will, from now on, become more and more important in a child's pre-school life. The baby's play is far simpler than that of the older child, and he requires very little material to satisfy his imaginative needs; but that material must have the right qualities. A doll should be unbreakable, neither too large nor too small, just medium sized for a small person of eighteen months; it need have no clothes since at eighteen months one is not concerned with dressing or undressing, but it must have something to be wrapped up, or tucked up, in; it must have a bed or pram, and boxes make perfectly good beds or prams. A baby will be content wrapping or unwrapping, tucking up and untucking a doll, for a very long time. I once watched a little girl of twenty months in a war nursery taking a doll out of a bed-box and putting it in again repeatedly for half an hour; I do not know how much longer she continued this game, for I had to leave after the half-hour and she was still busily doing it. Woolly animals are not substitutes for dolls; the only animal which children will accept and allow to take the place of a doll in their games is a teddy bear or a Koala bear; children all need dolls—they are essential, but other woolly animals are not essential, though children will enjoy having a few. It is also important to remember that boys want and need dolls just as much as girls. Doll play satisfies certain fundamental needs of a child; one is the desire to be grown-up, which is strong in a healthy child; it is unhealthy for children not to wish to grow up; in playing with dolls a child satisfies this wish in phantasy, and this is a great help so long as imaginative play does not take the place of other, constructive, play in the real world. The other need which is satisfied by doll's play is an emotional one; if you observe a small child playing with his doll you will soon notice that the doll is made to do and say those things which the child has either done or wanted to do and which bring him into conflict with the adult world or which he knows are considered wrong to do; the doll is then punished, frequently with severity or in ways in which he, the child, has never been treated by adults himself. In fact, the child works out his own emotional conflicts and difficulties on his doll; this is both a relief and a help to him in dealing with his own difficulties in real life, and we should not prevent him from doing this or even make him feel he is behaving badly when he treats his doll in this way. If we do we are only increasing his difficulties and intensifying his feeling of guilt over wrong behaviour. How often have I heard a grown-up telling a little child it is very unkind and wrong to spank dolly? He should be free to beat his dolls as he chooses, so long, of course, as he does not really damage them.

Babyhood

When X was just two years old the family moved house. Up till then she had been an excellent sleeper, but now she suddenly took to waking early, and then earlier and finally in the middle of the night. Her parents did not understand that this was an expression of her anxiety at the strange new environment; they thought it simply contrariness and naughtiness on her part. She insisted that she should come into her parents bedroom and they insisted equally strongly that she should not. They were *not* going to spoil her. The upshot of the disagreement was that the neighbour complained of the noise! So when X woke and started to cry she was moved with her cot into another room, away from the neighbours, where she continued to cry. The second day after this happened X took her doll after breakfast, put it into its pram, pushed the pram into the room into which her cot had been moved and said very firmly, 'bad, bad, go bath'. (The room happened to be the bathroom.) She returned to her nursery, waited a minute or two and then went back into the bathroom. She came out pushing the pram and saying soothingly 'good dolly, no cry'. The parents kept up their attempt for two weeks to 'break' her of her 'habit' of waking too early. Then they gave in because they were all at breaking point, including X, who had become, from a laughing happy child, a querulous, whining baby. She kept up her game with the doll during the whole two weeks, but the day the parents stopped moving the cot and took her into their room the game stopped also. In a few days X was once more sleeping soundly until 6.30 or 7 a.m.

EARLY DISCIPLINE

During the second year a baby certainly begins to understand something of the activity of adults; he quickly learns that 'no' and a shake of the head mean that grown-ups don't like what he is doing and that 'yes' and a smile mean the opposite. Of the two he usually has far more experience of the 'no' than of the 'yes', so it is not surprising that he learns and uses the 'no' more quickly himself. But the fact that he understands that much is no reason for our using this method of discipline. So long as a baby cannot under-stand a reason for either doing or not doing an action, it is not only useless our attempting to instil discipline by some kind of fear, it is very dangerous. If he is constantly checked he may become timid and unwilling to do anything or he may become aggressive and negative in his behaviour. How then can he be prevented from doing damage to himself and other people and things? There are two ways in which this can be done. In the first we can, by careful planning, when and where he is at large, arrange the environment so that as little as possible is within his reach which he may not handle.

The other is being as gentle and kind to him as possible when we do have to stop him or take something away from him; we can also distract his attention by giving him something he may have, by doing something with him or giving him something special to do for us. Fortunately very young children *can* easily be distracted to something new.

MEALS

Another aspect of early behaviour which adults find difficult to deal with is meal-times. Generally speaking the trouble begins when solid foods have been introduced to the child's diet and he is able and anxious to hold and use his spoon. But it may begin much earlier if weaning has not been carred out sufficiently slowly or left sufficiently late. We all know that whenever possible breast feeding is

the best for a baby. In any case, whether the child is breast
or bottle fed, his need to suck, often well into the second
year, should be respected. Even after a milk feed has been
dropped such as at the midday meal, the baby should be
allowed, if he so wants it, to have a little comforting suck
at breast or bottle after the meal, in the same way as an
older child may be given a sweet to finish off with. The
baby will, of his own accord, wean himself of his need to
suck when he is ready for it. If he is allowed to satisfy this
need for as long as he feels it he is more likely to retain
his pleasure in food of all kinds and not become a 'problem
eater' and to welcome the new foods as they are introduced
into his diet.

So long as he is being fed by adults a baby does not get
'messy' at meal-times. But as soon as he can use his hands,
and certainly as soon as he can use a spoon, everything is
changed. From then on, unless mother or nurse is willing
to accept a real mess, meals will become a misery instead
of a pleasure. For a baby a meal is no different from any
other activity except that it includes eating the food, as
well as playing with it! If he is to retain his pleasure and
interest in his food he must be allowed to handle it and
try to feed himself—sometimes the best thing to do is to
have two spoons—one for him and one for the mother.
While he is busy experimenting with his spoon she will
probably be able to get quite a lot of food into his mouth.
It is no good trying to 'make' baby eat something he does
not want or more than he wants. If it comes to a tussle
the baby will always win, anyway, sometimes after a great
deal of harm has been done to everyone's temper.

Small children tend to have violent likes and dislikes with
regard to foods, which come and go with no apparent
explanations. When they suddenly refuse rice pudding
which has been a favourite until then, the best thing is to

accept the fact, leave rice puddings out of their diet for a week or so, and then reintroduce them. One of the secrets of having a good 'eater' is to introduce as many varied things as early as possible in a baby's life, in very small quantities and frequently, so that he becomes used to all sorts of tastes and feels before he is really conscious of what is happening. I believe if babies were given carrots, cauliflowers and cabbage stalks to chew instead of rusks they would eat vegetables much better than they usually do when they grow older.

Chapter Two

THE NURSERY YEARS

2–6 *Years*

LEARNING THROUGH PLAY

THE beginning of the third year marks the end of one clear stage of life. Babyhood is definitely over. The normal healthy child has achieved the upright posture and human gait, the use of his hands, but above all the beginning of speech and with it self-consciousness and consciousness of others as separate beings.

Nursery School age in England is held to be roughly from two to five years, for compulsory school age is five. In recent years it has been recognised that most children are not ready for formal work in the 3 Rs until they are over six and that nursery or kindergarten activities are the best until the end of the sixth year. The 3 Rs are essentially the tools for future learning, at second hand, of a mass of knowledge which man has accumulated in the course of thousands of years of existence, and which each child could not possibly recapitulate for himself. This learning at second hand can only be successful if a child has had sufficient opportunity of learning through his own direct experience something of the nature of all those aspects of the world which he will, later on, be required to learn through books and teachers. If all the possible time is given to free experimental play activity, both individual and social, a small child still has little time, in comparison with all he has to learn, to practice the skills he must master in those four short years, particularly when one remembers how unskilled and ignorant he is at two in comparison with an adult!

During these four nursery years the child will master all the skills he requires for adult activities, and he will do this almost entirely through his play. He will learn a great deal about the function and use of everyday things in his environment and he will learn many natural laws. This he will learn as much through social play as through his own individual investigations. But he will, once more, only do this if the adult world provides him with the opportunity, the material and the environment.

Once a child has learnt to walk and his growing understanding and curiosity lead him to investigate all he can see, his world of experience is enlarged. From now onward for many years there are two worlds for him, that of out-of-doors and that of indoors. They are both equally important.

OUTDOOR OCCUPATIONS

Physical skills and balance

From two years onwards physical skills will remain of predominant importance, but the third year is the one in which physical balance and co-ordination are really mastered. After that it is a question of finer details, perfection of skill, increase in speed, etc.

A two-year-old, confident of his ability to stand, walk, and run should begin to concentrate on greater elaboration.

A toddler who is fortunate enough to meet a slide, a climbing frame, or even a swing, will, if he has been allowed

IIIa. Water Play. You learn a great deal
from the greatest fun

IIIb. Slide. You require confidence

IVb. Ropeladder. Climbing is one of childhood's joys and is most educational

IVa. Gardening. This is an adult skill which all children enjoy

to develop freely in the past, take to it with delight. He will try to balance-walk on planks, he will climb over low fences, jump off tree-trunks. J was just two years old when I moved my nursery school into new premises; there was an iron staircase leading from the classroom into the garden. J was very attracted by the banisters of this staircase and spent a great deal of time in the garden climbing up the stairs on the outside of the railings. There were twenty steps to the top; it took a long time to climb to the top, but she never stopped half-way, nor did she ever slip.

The other children were not slow to follow, and soon all of them, from two-year-olds upwards, were climbing quickly and surely.

All the equipment needed by a two-year-old is as necessary for a three-year-old. But a three-year-old will naturally go farther and do more.

He will be able to ride a tricycle if he is given one. A proper tricycle is much better than a kiddy-car; the latter upsets easily and more often than not the pedals will not turn easily. A tricycle is usually much easier to pedal, and as pedalling is a difficult accomplishment, anyway, it should be made as easy as possible. From three onwards almost any child enjoys a machine it can ride. Carts in which they can pull each other along are also useful. Old prams are ideal for this purpose.

Bats and balls to hit and kick and throw are useful now. Balls should be large and light, bats small and light. Reins for playing horses are also good for running practice.

Four-year-old girls and boys are very conscious of no longer being babies. They can not only walk and run with complete confidence, talk fairly fluently, if with a restricted vocabulary, but they have already achieved a fair degree of control over their environment.

The effect of this rapid growth in physical control and

The Nursery Years

achievement shows itself in a desire and need for daring exploits, particularly in their outdoor life. Dangerous and exciting acts, such as climbing to the very top of high railings, balancing along the narrow edge of a low wall, swinging as high as possible on a swing, shooting down a slide head first—all these are the ambition of any healthy and normal four-year-old.

It was among the four-year-olds in the nursery school that we listened most frequently to the 'look what I can do, you can't do that; I can because I'm bigger than you', and the younger child was treated to a hair-raising shoot down the slide.

In the garden there was a very convenient tree growing against a wall; the five-year-olds were very fond of climbing it and then running along the wall and jumping off. For them this was an easy feat, but for the four-year-olds it was different. Yet they nearly all attempted it.

One little girl could not reach the lowest branch; she struggled and stretched, but it was no good. A bright companion suggested a box. This seemed a good idea, so she dragged one up, and climbed on to the branch, and then with great difficulty she bridged the gap between the last branch and the wall. There was not one child between four and six who did not at least attempt that climb. Those who found the balancing along the top of the wall rather frightening were given a hand by a friendly adult.

A child's physical development, his agility and confidence will be greatly increased and very much advanced by the frequent use of such material as a slide, swings, and other gymnastic apparatus already mentioned. Rope ladders can also be added to the number, and rings, for a four-year-old.

All children of this age should naturally be free to climb trees and railings and walls, to balance and swing on anything available for that purpose in their environment.

Tricycles are still very useful to learn new tricks on, and to ride about fast and furiously on.

Besides climbing, swinging, jumping, etc., a two-year-old enjoys pushing things about, loading and unloading vans and carts.

Play equipment

All toys for this purpose, particularly garden ones, should be strong and large enough for the child to get real satisfaction from filling them up with sand, leaves or earth. They must be sufficiently strong for a child to sit and be pushed about in, for children will always use them for this purpose if playmates are present. Sand and water are essential playthings for almost all ages after two years. Mugs, jugs, pots and pans, spades, buckets, all these are admirable garden toys for a sand-pit, but real ones should always be used, not miniature doll's things. It is always worth spending a little more money to buy really strong spades, buckets and all gardening tools. If a child breaks his tools easily he is discouraged in his work and encouraged in carelessness and destructiveness.

A sand-pit and an old bath in the garden are also essential; gymnastic apparatus such as a slide, swing, climbing frame are also ideal if you can afford them. A child who is given freedom to experiment in these ways develops mental as well as physical stability and confidence. A child need not have to possess a climbing frame to have experience in climbing; railings, gates, ladders, trees, growing and felled, are usually found somewhere within the child's reach, and if you have no swing or slide in your garden there is sure to be one in a public playground fairly near.

A little girl of three came to my nursery school; she was so nervous that she shivered whenever she was spoken to. She never spoke above a whisper, she wet herself continuously. She did not dare go into the garden from the classroom because the way was down an iron staircase.

She was too frightened to take any play material for herself and fell down far more frequently than a three-year-old should. At the end of a month at school she ventured up the outside of the staircase, tried the rope ladder, swung on rings, and went shooting down the slide. At the same time the shivering stopped, the whisper changed into a shout, and her knickers were never wet. She had gained confidence.

Almost any kitchen and household utensils are good for garden use when they can be spared. If you have a garden, let your child play in it frequently, either alone or with a companion of his own age. It is much better than going for walks all the time. Let him scramble about, balance on old planks. When he does go for a walk let him run where he will, climb, jump and swing.

In the summer a sun-suit, water, sand, and a pail or so will make a two-year-old (or any-other-year-old for that matter) happy for hours. If the garden hose is available too, then it is almost heaven. A garden is an entirely different place to play in from a nursery, or any other room in a house, and it has certain qualities about it which are absolutely essential to a growing child.

Living things

The usefulness of out of doors is not, of course, restricted to play with large equipment, such as climbing frames, bicycles, swings, etc. It has a quality which is both exclusive to itself and of fundamental importance. It harbours living, growing things, plants and animals. Its importance cannot be overestimated for it is from nature itself that children first learn its laws, and gain the interest they needs must have if they are to profit later from their nature lessons in school. A child that has never seen a worm, a beetle or an ant cannot be expected to show a thrill at learning their life story from a teacher as he sits unrestfully at his desk in a crowded classroom. Children's curiosity about the moving world of living creatures can easily be seen by the long and concentrated attention they give to all the forms of life they meet in the garden. They will show astonishing patience and be as quiet as a mouse while they watch an ant drag an enormous egg across the path, or a beetle struggling to get on to its feet again. There is quite literally no end to the things they can discover about this earth of ours. They watch, they follow, they collect any insects that cannot escape, they ask endless questions about their treasures, they show great delight and interest in 'caring' for them, even if this interest does not last more than a few hours! When my school was evacuated during the last war we had a country house with a large field in which grew a great deal of tansy. In August black and yellow striped caterpillars feed on this plant and our field had hundreds of these caterpillars. We always knew when the caterpillars were about because the house became full of them. The children filled their pockets, their hands and every empty box they could lay their hands on with them. We found caterpillars under pillows, inside drawers, in the cupboards and the crockery. Children will investigate everything they find, soil, stones, sand, sticks, the flowers, fruits and seeds of all the plants and trees. They will want to know the why and wherefore of everything, and if they are given the freedom to investigate and experiment they will answer many of their own questions.

It is this direct experience of living matter which will sow the seeds of later interest and hence of knowledge. The experience of the nursery years must be the child's own choice. The adult world is only responsible for providing the opportunity. If there is no garden, and how many millions of families in our urban communities are deprived of this necessity, all available parks should be used and the children encouraged to use their ears and eyes.

Naturally all gardens are not equally suitable for small children. A formal garden full of carefully tended beds with rare and beautiful flowers, small clipped lawns bordered by gravel paths with clipped box or yew hedges, is not the right thing. The best garden of all is one in which there is plenty of relatively uncultivated land, big lawns, shrubberies in which children can hide and play, trees to climb, a good rubbish and compost heap, a few flowers, a few vegetable beds, enough to interest a growing child, but not to occupy most of the space. Children also need a corner where they can do anything they like, including making a mess; they need a sand-pit as well. If the sand is just loose in a corner of the garden it is more likely to be scattered about; this means the sand will disappear and the garden become untidy. If the adults care for the garden, work in it, and take pleasure in growing plants the children will tend to imitate them and this goes a long way to encourage thoughtfulness and tidiness. On the whole small children prefer carts, cans, trucks, etc., to wheelbarrows to play with. But if the gardener is working with a barrow it is quite a different matter. The children will all want a barrow to trundle round after the gardener, and that is as it should be.

One very important aspect of outdoor play is the opportunity it gives for the most varied kinds of collections. It is not only little boys who proverbially fill their pockets with the strangest assortment of stones, sticks, empty matchboxes, ends of string, bits of paper, conkers, fir cones, berries, etc. Little girls collect with as much alacrity. The garden is full of things which are 'lying about' in the most inviting fashion, from earthworms and snails to flints and pebbles, and the grass mowings thrown carelessly on the compost heap.

The baby up to two and a half or three collects as a matter of course with no ulterior motive behind it; he automatically picks up everything which catches his eye, like a magpie. But after the age of three, collections are also made with a purpose; either for tea parties and domestic play generally, or for loading and unloading goods in trains, vans, trucks, etc. Not only are these collections most useful and satisfactory for imaginative play, they quite unconsciously and indirectly forward the children's general knowledge; the desire to collect leads them to observe, study and learn from the very objects they are collecting, and this is a far surer way of obtaining knowledge than a nature lesson would be!

The five-year-old

At five years old, children, and particularly boys, become more ambitious as regards their games. They want to be able to play what the big boys and girls play, namely, football, rounders, cricket. The possession of a football, bat, stumps, rubber ball instead of a cricket ball, or rounders stick (preferably a racket instead) is usually prized above other things. Naturally the children find it difficult not only to do the correct things but also to co-operate and keep the rules. But the desire to do so helps them to learn the difficult lessons of self-control and sacrifice of personal wishes and aims, for the common purpose of the group.

This ambition is also very helpful in acquiring certain physical skills, such as throwing, catching, kicking, batting. And it is well worth while to encourage a five-year-old in these things even though his attempts are very crude and short-lived.

The Nursery Years

A well-developed and healthy five-year-old should enjoy climbing; and one who has had a climbing frame at home or at a nursery school should be an expert tree climber.

I used to take my eldest group of nursery school children, those from five plus to six plus, on to Hampstead Heath nearly every morning. The favourite occupations were (1) tree climbing, (2) paddling in the streams. We were very lucky in that Hampstead Heath has a good stock of excellent trees for climbing, and few of the children did not reach the tops. I even once had a keeper after me for allowing children under my care to do dangerous things! Yet the children were always cautious and we never had an accident.

A child who has had a tricycle for some time and ridden it a great deal is quite ready to attempt balancing on a Fairy cycle at five if he is tall enough to reach the pedals. Jane started riding a tricycle when she was two and a half; by the time she was five she was very tired of tricycles and begged for a Fairy cycle—but being very small she could not reach the pedals. So she had to wait, but at six she learnt to ride in a few weeks.

The value of scraps and odds and ends, particularly for dressing-up, increases with the age of the children. Already at five, make-believe games have become very serious and complicated, and have improved in technique and elaborateness. Pretend games out of doors, particularly in the summer, offer much more attraction and excitement than they do indoors.

So wise parents provide the wherewithal for tents, planks to build tree houses in the lower branches, and old clothes for dressing-up. This, of course, is in addition to the things which have already been mentioned for younger children.

The Nursery Years

The two-year-old's needs

From two to six years indoor play equipment varies chiefly in quantity and complexity. The younger child is still concerned with developing his five senses and the older, say from four and a half or five to six is consolidating his knowledge and beginning to learn different skills, such as drawing and painting recognizable shapes, cutting with scissors, making a weaving or sewing needle go in and out correctly. Toys should help to encourage thought, effort, constructiveness and feed the imagination. The younger child is still largely unsociable, that is, his chief occupation is to be doing things and investigating his own little material world.

The material which helps the progress of sense development should be more complicated and difficult than that used for children under two years. A child should not have much of this material; two or three fitting toys such as the Abbatt picture trays, or Montessori cylinders, are quite sufficient. The most important point is that all this type of material should be self explanatory so that the child can play alone.

From two onwards the chief motive force behind all a child's activities is a desire to do as the adults do. He wants to sweep, dust, clean, and do all the other household things which are done by grown-ups. This desire should not be discouraged. He should be given the wherewithal to do these things; these tools should, like garden toys, be strong and efficient for the job; it is no good a child being given a doll's broom which breaks the moment he begins to sweep! He should be shown how to do things and allowed to practice, and make mistakes.

Do not forbid him to clean the bath because it makes a mess; too much checking and forbidding either kills his healthy natural interest or else turns the child into an obsessive water maniac! A little boy of two who had never been allowed to use water alone or wash his own hands came to school. When he found a sink with hot and cold water in the classroom, he ran the water and washed his hands for most of the mornings for nearly a whole term.

Toys such as trucks, trains, carts, building blocks of all kinds, serve a double purpose, particularly those trains and trucks which are put together from separate parts. They encourage thought, construction and effort, and they are perfect for imaginative play. The best building blocks are the large hollow plywood ones, for with them one can build a house, boat, or aeroplane in which one can sit.

Pull-about toys like trains and carts are very popular, because walking about is still rather a great pleasure, and loading and unloading is a favourite past-time.

Painting, drawing, modelling are occupations a two-year-old will take to with pleasure. They serve several purposes. The child learns to use tools such as a brush or a pencil, he improves his hand and eye co-ordination, and increases his visual acuity and colour sense. Through his imagination he can satisfy his power sense even though the scribbles he produces have no recognizable shapes. He also satisfies a very deep need to express his feelings and work out his problems and difficulties. Clay has a very special function, similar to that of water and sand; not only can they be all used for creative purposes but also for destructive purposes. Destructiveness seems to be inherent in the human make-up, and it is also a means of venting feeling and emotion which might otherwise be either brought down on the heads of others or bottled up. Both these latter are harmful ways of dealing with emotional difficulties, and the outlet afforded by water, sand, clay and earth is a very necessary one. It is comforting for the small child, and indeed essential to his ultimate happiness, to find that when he has sufficiently destroyed, i.e. poured all the water away, broken all the sand pies, pounded and shredded a lump of clay, he has actually done no harm, and that all can be once more restored to its first condition.

The best colours to use for painting are poster paints, in jars, with big brushes and large sheets of paper. Dryad paints are particularly good. Easels have recently become popular in nursery schools and some homes; but I have found the children get upset and discouraged when the paint trickles down away from the spot on which it was generously splashed. I find a large sheet of paper spread on the floor or a low table is much more convenient. Too many colours should not be given. The three primary— red, blue, and yellow—are sufficient for a two-year-old; he will then be able to make experiments in mixing and see what new colours he can make himself. If poster paints are too expensive, water colours or powder paints should be used. In all cases the paint should be mixed with water in small jars by the adults so that they are ready for use. The children should experiment themselves in mixing colours. On no condition should paint boxes with small hard squares of solid paint and very small brushes be given to children. They are quite useless for painting a proper picture and are consequently most disappointing and discouraging.

Ordinary potter's clay is the best medium for modelling for small children; it is not greasy, and will wash off anything easily. It is cheap; it can be painted when dry and made to look like real grown-up pottery. Dough made from flour and water mixed to a smooth paste with powder paint to give it colour is an excellent alternative to clay for younger children. It is easier to keep in malleable condition and easier for the children to knead and roll out. If a pinch of salt is added to the mixture it will keep for at least a week or longer. It should be kept covered with a damp cloth when not in use.

Scissors, too, can be used by a child under three; although he cannot cut properly be can begin to learn how to hold and use the scissors and possibly cut paper. Scissors should have rounded tops. Paper and scissors all afford opportunity for useful destruction; a most satisfying occupation is to cut up a piece of paper into minute scraps, and if a child has not yet learned to use scissors, tearing the paper is equally satisfactory.

The older nursery child

All the play material which the two-year-old uses and enjoys remains useful till the end of the nursery years, except perhaps the simpler picture-trays, puzzles and fitting toys. Yet even these have their uses, for the older children sometimes grow weary of playing with equipment which requires constant effort and concentration; they need, occasionally, to relax and rest a little and also to show how clever they can be with little effort. So they sometimes like to take out 'easy' things which they can do quickly and well and show off their achievement.

Besides the toys of the two-year-olds, children from three to five need more elaborate and detailed equipment. Where the smaller child only requires a doll, with a wrapper, a pram or a bed, the older ones want dolls' clothes, a Wendy house, a tea set and pots and pans. A two-year-old will be very well occupied pouring water from one can into another or simply hitting and spashing the water with his hands or a stick; four and five-year-olds are quite able to study the displacement of water by heavy bodies which sink, find out what happens when you blow air into water, and the excitingly different properties of dry and wet sand. If they are not given the opportunity of doing these things, handling the different tools to make these discoveries, their play will not teach them as much as it can, and they will be bored. As they grow older all the play material must be more elaborate and more detailed. For water play they require bottles of all shapes and sizes, wide and narrow funnels, rubber tubing, tins with holes in them; holes in the bottoms and holes in the sides so that the children can see how differently the water comes out. They need all kinds of light things and all kinds of heavy things so that they can find out what sinks and what floats. Similarly they need more things for their sand play.

Fortunately much of this equipment is cheap and easy to get. Empty jars, and tins, old spoons and forks, stones, sticks, flowers and leaves to make gardens and villages in the sand pit; they all make useful equipment.

While building bricks and train sets remain as popular as ever, they will be used in more elaborate and difficult games. Combined with 'dinky' cars, buses, farm-yard animals, traffic signals, etc., children will use them to lay out whole villages, or the countryside, and very seriously play out in make-believe the actions they have witnessed, or thought they have witnessed, in the world outside.

Fantasy Play

The vast realm of make-believe becomes important as soon as a child can begin to speak and realize his helplessness and inferiority in comparison with the grown-up world.

The dominant wish of any healthy child is to be grown-up, to do all the things he cannot or is forbidden to do; to wield the—to him—unlimited power of adults, who cause the magic of food and clothing and other creative acts, who get up and go to bed when they choose and come and go as they choose. It is this wish which stimulates his interest in all household tasks and activities and gives him the energy and capacity to learn how to do them.

A small child is, however, still too immature and in-experienced to be able to do in reality all the things adults do. So he satisfies his need by carrying out many of these acts in imaginative play. This make-believe finds its ex-pression in almost all the small child's activities, but those which are the most satisfying for this need are the games of mother and father, centred in the Wendy house with dolls; ship, trains, aeroplanes with their crews, centred in constructions with building bricks, planks, crates, etc., and last but not least, the floor layout of village, farm, zoo or roads and traffic with the dinky toy material.

Make-believe play fulfils two objects. It is used as a compensation for being dependent, and, relative to adults, ignorant and helpless, but it is also one of the most im-portant ways of learning new skills, practising old ones and puzzling out new situations and experiences which the child has met in the outside world. Because the drive behind the play is the wish to be adult, the child puts effort and thought into his activity. It nearly always requires planning, judgement and comparison.

The younger the child the simpler the make-believe play. At no stage in the nursery years is expensive material re-quired. Large costly dolls with magnificent clothing are not favourites; smaller, softer ones, which can be taken to bed and easily cuddled are far better even for the six-year-olds. Home-made dolls and clothes which a child has watched being made bring a greater pride of ownership and also awakens a desire to learn the necessary skill to make them himself. The child will also show more care

The Nursery Years

and respect for the toys, for he will, in fact, love them much more.

A clothes horse, particularly a large three-sided one, makes an excellent Wendy house; if the children watch the grown-ups tie or sew a piece of coarse canvas on to it, leaving a gap for a door and window, and then sew up a door curtain and window curtains, they will appreciate and cherish it much more.

A Wendy house and furniture which father and mother have made are also more loved and valued.

Woolly animals, particularly teddy bears, are loved just as much as dolls. Children should not, however, be given many of these; one or two are sufficient to satisfy even a five-year-old and act as a stimulus to play. More often than not I have noticed children have one favourite animal or doll (sometimes two) and they play with these however many others, finer, shinier, larger, and more gorgeously dressed, they may be given.

J. loved her teddy bear from the age of two (she had him on her first birthday but did not look at him till she was two)—she loved him passionately and exclusively for four years; then came a tree bear and she loved them both devotedly for many years, long after both had all the fur hugged off them. She had dolls and other animals given her in plenty, and we had to give them away.

A boy had a rag doll whose name was Bess; she went everywhere with him, all day, all night; when he was five she had no head left and was shabby, to say the least; but she was the only one he loved.

And the moral of those two tales is, 'don't give more dolls or animals when the child is happy with those he has'. If you intend giving a doll or animal to a child who has not got a beloved creature, find out first what kind he likes best; for children have very strong likes and dislikes.

The Nursery Years

When giving dolls' furniture or household articles never give anything elaborate or luxurious, but always give things which can be really used. Dolls' houses are also excellent food for the imagination. Naturally a home-made one is best; and the best one has only sufficient furnishings to stimulate a desire to make more properties yourself. Expensive and elaborate ones are so full of ingenious devices that there is no room left for invention or imagaination when once they have been examined all over.

A small boy of my acquaintance had one shabby old dolls' house which had been passed on to him from some-one else. He was so fond of it that a doting grandfather decided he should have a really fine dolls' house instead. When the new one arrived the small boy said: 'It's much too grand for my dollies' (he had a very mixed crowd of small objects which had once been dollies) 'and they like their own house best.' And that was the end of the new dolls' house.

Dolls' houses are also a good incentive to making things, such as match-box furniture, woven mats, cardboard chairs and tables, painting and decorating. And five-year-olds can make quite a lot when they try hard enough and have the wherewithal to make the things.

Only a little is needed by the two-year-old. As the children grow in age, and experience and skills, they require more equipment. Here again it need not be expensive. A few cups and saucers and plates, empty jars and little boxes and bottles, a few old pots and pans no longer required in the kitchen; lids of small tins can be painted to make plates and saucers and dishes.

Imaginative play, from three years onwards, seems to be slightly different for boys and girls. Whether this is the effect of social attitudes which tend on the whole to expect boys to be masculine minded and girls to be artistic and doll-minded, or whether it is a real sex-determined differ-ence, it is impossible to know at present. The fact remains that boys tend to show more interest in mechanical toys, engines, aeroplanes, motor-cars and buses than girls. They centre their scientific curiosity and their imaginative play around engines of one kind or another. The best kind to get is a simple, solidly built wooden type, without elaborate clockwork or electric mechanism but which rolls well on four wheels. Wood, here again, is the best material. Trains for two-year-olds are best without wheels, and the separate sections should couple in the easiest way, one having a knob which fits into a groove in another. Older children need more complicated things, tenders, trucks, carriages which are different from each other and which are open and hollow so that they can be loaded. Trains will then be combined with constructions made with building bricks and quite elaborate games can be played.

Girls seem on the whole to prefer animals and dolls for their imaginative games, which centre more round family life. Boys do, however, play these games, and it is as wrong to discourage them by deriding such occupations for them, as it is to discourage scientific and mechanical interests in girls.

Dramatic play

There is one other aspect of make-believe which plays an important part in childhood and which satisfies more than any other the wish to be grown-up. It grows quite naturally out of group play of mothers and fathers, engine drivers, pilots, etc., when the adults give the children old clothes for dressing up in. Already three-year-olds show the first signs of this play by wrapping themselves in what they can find lying about and using material which the environment provides. Chairs and tables will be used to

make a house; a rug thrown over the top provides a roof.
Old boxes serve excellently for beds, building blocks and
planks will make furniture. This is the best material possible together with other playthings named already, engines, dolls, etc. These all provide food for the imagination
and invention. Here is the beginning of dramatic play,
dressing-up and acting.

Children love dressing-up, particularly when they are in
groups of two or more. But they will only do so if they
are stimulated and encouraged by the provision of material.
A few very dramatically inclined children will have sufficient
drive and initiative to seek out the wherewithal to make-
believe, but the vast majority will not.

One morning I called on a friend in Cambridge. As I
went upstairs I tripped over an old silk skirt, and loud
voices from the children's room announced that something
was in the air. My friend's two children had a small neighbour in, and in the midst of a whole heap of old clothes,
shoes, and hats they were rehearsing a fairy-tale. It was
not a proper play, produced by an adult, nor was it acted
in front of a large audience; they were merely amusing
themselves making up the play as they went along. This
sort of occupation played a large rôle in these children's
lives, because they were encouraged in it and given plenty
of old scraps to play with.

If there is a dressing-up cupboard or chest of drawers,
set aside for this particular purpose, and lovely, fascinating
scraps of material, old clothes, and old-fashioned clothes
are occasionally added to the stock, it is a very dull child
who will not respond.

There is also the endless delight of making your own
properties, and even a four-year-old can make something,
particularly if he has always free use of various tools. Hats,
belts, crowns, swords and daggers are easily made out of

paper and cardboard (thin enough for small children to cut) and children will for a short space of time prefer their own home-made properties to other dressing-up clothes. It is a great mistake to buy children ready-made fancy-dress clothes; they will get more pleasure out of clothes made at home with their own help. It will also encourage their desire to make things themselves.

But if an elaborate fancy-dress costume is a hindrance to dramatic creativeness, the gift of a box of make-up, on the contrary, is a very great incentive. This, however, should be treated with respect. It is professional equipment and children must realize this, much as it may tempt them to mess about with it for fun. In giving this type of material to children it is important, from the educational standpoint, to see that it is used seriously for its correct purpose. This does not lower its value in the children's eyes; on the contrary, it enhances it and makes the children put added effort and concentration into their acting. And naturally this is all to the good.

Learning adult skills

If imaginative play is a roundabout method of learning to be adult, actually doing the things grown-up people do is certainly not. Young children are able to do far more than most people think. If a two-year-old is given the opportunity of carrying, pouring, mixing, sweeping, stirring, opening, shutting and doing all the thousand and one everyday acts which his mother has to carry out, he will learn very quickly to do these things and to do them carefully and skilfully. It is not difficult to plan his training so that he can do the minimum of harm during the learning process. If he carries potatoes and not eggs, pours water rather than milk, puts away objects which he cannot break easily, no great damage will be done. A child needs the tools for many of these activities and he should have them, from the age of two upwards. Whether they are brushes and brooms or hammers and saws they must be strong and useful for their special purpose. Constant practice with the household tools during these nursery years makes for perfection, as our old motto tells us. As the years go by skill and understanding grow with experience. A six-year-old who has had a hammer and saw at a work bench for several years has become something of a carpenter. He can make very recognizable boats and aeroplanes, not to mention daggers and swords. And here again it is the wish to become adult which gives drive and energy to the work.

Make-believe play is a compensation for being weak and young; learning how to do things helps you on your way, but because a child is still small he does, in practice, achieve but little of the ends his mother reaches. It is sometimes most discouraging even for a five-or six-year-old, so he needs the sympathy and help of the adults.

Creative experience

Creative play with sand, paint, clay, building bricks, constructional toys as well as carpentry provide just that element of successful achievement which children need so much to feel that they also are able to make things, as their parents do.

The younger the child the less important this need is. The two-year-old is too busy exploring the material at hand to 'do' anything with it. But from three onwards most children know enough about the quality of sand, paint, etc., to be able to use them. The delight of making something is very strong and gives the child the interest to concentrate and work hard. Constructional toys, such as Mini-bricks and Tinkertoys, are very popular with four and five-year-olds. These toys require skill with fingers, judgement and planning to create something the child had in mind. It is not necessary, however, to buy such constructional toys, for it is possible to make suitable material out of cotton reels, oddments of wood and dowel rod. Round and flat bits of wood which can be held together by different lengths of dowel rod form the basis of such toys as 'Tinkertoy' and 'Pick-a-Brick'; children make endless things from such material, boats, aeroplanes, guns, cars, etc.

Play with sand, clay, paint becomes more elaborate and more skilful with the years, but it always remains essential. It will remain so until adolescence. The sand should be good washed sand and the children should be encouraged to undertake difficult and elaborate constructions involving the building of castles, moats, bridges, tunnels, tracks, roads, villages, with the imaginative use of every kind of material which nature provides, such as leaves, berries, nuts, flowers, sticks, stones and shells. All sand toys, just as gardening tools, should be strong and useful.

When the two-year-old has learnt just what paints are and how you splash or dab them on to paper he has become the proficient three-year-old who knows how to hold a paint brush and how to make real lines and circles—not just scrubbings! By the time he has reached his sixth year his painting has taken on real shape, there is no unsightly scrubbing with a half-dry brush and much effort and trouble are put into achieving a real engine or house or what you will. All through the nursery years the key to his painting is large brushes, large pieces of paper and not more than the three primary colours with black and white. Just as skill in building, painting, modelling grow with age, so does the ability to use tools such as scissors, paste, needle and wool. From four onwards children's manual skill is sufficiently good for them to be able to use their hands for 'making' things. It is at this stage that scrap material becomes very useful indeed and will remain so until childhood is left behind. Wise parents provide all the scrap they can from empty match-boxes and dead matches to cornflake boxes and ice-cream cartons (how much more useful for these to be used for a creative purpose than to be left lying about in parks!). In fact there is little, other than jagged or rusty tins, of all the junk which is daily accumulated in a house which cannot be profitably used by small children; bits of string, sticks, remnants from dressmaking. This capacity to create out of odds and ends exercises skill, imaginativeness and ingenuity in children. It does not appear out of the blue. It has to be fostered and cultivated, encouraged and helped, for it requires effort, concentration and thought; all qualities which we wish our children to develop and which are difficult to achieve. Our part in the process is to provide the material, take an interest in the children's work, give helpful suggestions from time to time and praise the achievement, however crude it may be.

Children who have had plenty of experience with all kinds of handwork materials and opportunity to use fingers skilfully are able to begin sewing and weaving when they are about five years old. Here again it is the desire to achieve adult skills which prompts them. As with any other new activity it must be started in the simplest and easiest way. Large rugwool needles and rug wool should be used with large-holed rug wool canvas; correct and tidy stitches should not be expected. It is sufficient that a small child should be prepared to put effort into learning a new skill and, if he is willing to cover a whole piece of canvas with his stitching, he should be praised; he will also have 'made' a real thing, a mat, and this achievement will encourage him to further effort. Similarly with weaving, a small frame made from four pieces of wood, a few nails on two opposite sides, a single strand of rug wool threaded across and the loom is ready. Rug wool and needle make it possible to weave a little mat almost in one sitting.

BOOKS

A child learns to speak by imitating the sounds he hears around him. As his interest in all the objects of his environment is aroused, so he learns to name them; he enjoys meeting familiar things, and recognizing them. It is at this point that picture books should enter his field of experience. To a child's vision the world is a vast place made up of a number of objects which he knows stading out against a general blurred background. It is these familiar objects which he loves to recognize. So a two-year-old should be given simple pictures of these objects; single objects presented as clearly and strikingly as possible are best. A small child cannot take in a mass of detail. Books of photographs of animals, of household articles—simple outline paintings with bright colours, and not too many of them—these are the things to aim at.

Picture books such as two-year-olds like are still popular, probably more so, at three and even four years. But for three-year-olds the pictures should be more detailed— instead of the likeness of a single object the picture should be a simple story-telling one; a simple action can be understood and it is exciting.

But here again the basic principle of simple, bold outline with a minimum of detail and shading gives the best result. A story book made up only of pictures—a short story at that—is just the thing for this age. Very simple stories can also be begun with three- to four-year-olds; the best are those of everyday activities told so as to bring in a maximum of repetition with a picture for each sentence. Simple animal stories, in which the animals talk and behave much as a small child does, are usually very popular. The text should always be within a three-year-old's vocabulary; sentences should be short and snappy; paragraphs should be short also, and the story should be action from beginning to end. Many books are brought out in large print, with a very few sentences printed on a page. This is an excellent idea, for it makes reading attractive and seems within the grasp of the toddler; it makes it delightful for the older ones who are just struggling to master the difficult art.

Nursery rhymes and simple, very jingly, poetry appeal to a child's natural sense of rhythm and song; he learns them by heart quite unconsciously, and they serve as a good basis for memory training, dance and mime.

Although picture books will continue to delight children of all ages, they are not sufficient in themselves for children over four. These need story books with real long stories, continuing from page to page, with frequent pictures to help the characters and action to appear more real and vivid to the child.

The content and style of writing are as important for first stories as they are for the more complex and sophisticated ones designed for older children. As regards content a story should have continuous action of a kind which is both understandable for, and exciting to, a four-year-old; action should also be quick, and the book should not have long descriptive passages. It should be about the things, people, and animals a child is interested in; they should act and speak in a way which is natural and normal to a four-year-old.

The language should be simple and direct; sentences should be short, and there should be a great deal of repetition and conversation. Condescension and smugness, puns, hints, and other subtleties either bewilder or annoy a small child. Adult humour also cuts no ice. Fun must be straightforward and primitive. Then there is a certain code of behaviour with which all stories must comply, and certain rules which must always be kept. Perhaps the most important is that 'they all lived happily ever after', in fact, the ending must be happy. The wicked must always receive their just punishment and the good be rewarded! Furthermore, if the story deals with 'good' and 'bad' these must be of the kind the child itself has experience of and can understand, questions of social behaviour on his own level.

A good example of what I mean is the story of Peter Rabbit; his mother forbade him to visit Mr. McGregor's garden and told him why he should not go. His greed led him to the inevitable consequence of illness, bed and camomile tea! The morals and ethics of story books, if they must have them, must be the ethics and morals practised in the child's own environment.

A wildly fantastic tale which could not occur in reality is just as exciting and enjoyable as a real story, provided the action and words within the framework given are strictly logical and reasonable from the child's point of view. For instance, it does not upset a little child at all to hear a duck talking, but if he talks badly or incongruously, then the child will think him 'stupid' and lose interest in the story. Last, but not least, stories should always be short; in fact, short enough to be finished in one reading, as children of this age cannot listen for more than about fifteen minutes.

Nursery rhymes and jingles are as popular with four-year-olds as with younger children; they can also listen to poetry so long as it is short, simple and with very marked rhythm and scansion.

The Nursery Years

Five-year-olds are nearly always ready for a story. And they want more content to their stories, more complication, more excitement than in the previous year. Plots can be more elaborate, they can be spun out longer. But the basic qualities of the style should remain the same. Repetition, lilt and rhythm make a great difference to a story at this age.

Fantasy tales

There are psychologists who say children should have, and in fact prefer, stories of the real everyday world in which they live, and that fairy-stories are bad for them. Personally I think this is definitely incorrect and wrong. Not that children don't like stories which might be true, or are actually true, of the world they know; they do, of course, like well-written ones very much; but fantasy life, as everyone knows, is not only very important in a young child's life, it is also intensely real. Provided a child is normally healthy and happily adjusted to reality, fantasy life has no harmful effect, but on the contrary is a great help in developing his creative and imaginative faculties. And fantasy stories are important, as is shown by the universal desire there is for them. Naturally there are good and bad stories of make-believe. Grimm's and Andersen's fairy tales are not on the whole suitable for children under six; nor are the majority of our own classic fairy tales, such as Lang's or folk stories or legends. They are all considerably too advanced and complicated, both in content and style; they are frequently very frightening and the imaginary creatures of fairy tales such as giants, witches, goblins and fairies have not yet entered into the fantasy world of the young child. There are, however, certain exceptions, which probably come immediately to the reader's mind: *The Three Bears, The Three Little Pigs, Little Red Riding Hood,*

The Little Red Hen are amongst the best known. Although many of them have what appear to be horrifying characters, most children do not seem to be in the least frightened by them. They are, however, among the simplest of our traditional fairy tales. There are also a number of folk stories which are short and simple enough for very young children, and some verge on rhymes, such as *The House that Jack Built*; most of them are of the repetitive type so common to folk-tales the world over, such as *The Ginger-Bread Boy* and *Billy Goat Gruff*. The best collection I know for five-year-olds (and six- and seven-year-olds for that matter) is that found in the Beacon Readers, Books 2, 3 and 4. *Picture Tales from the Russian*, by Valerie Garrick is another collection of folk-tales very simply told. The action is direct, the animals behave exactly like the human beings who tell the story, i.e. simple peasants who are very child-like. There is, as in our own folk-tales, frequent repetition in most of the stories, and many are so rhythmical in their form as to be nearly poetry.

This book, together with the 'Little Black Sambo' series and *Millions of Cats* by Wanda Gag, was definitely a favourite in my nursery school; many of the children knew the stories off by heart. Whenever a story was read there were continued interruptions such as 'Wasn't Bruin silly to be tricked like that?' or 'Mr. Sampson Cat did tell lies, didn't he?' These interruptions show how popular a story is.

On the whole, the favourite stories are not 'reality' ones but make-believe at this age. All the books mentioned so far are fantasy tales, and they and others like them were far more popular than the *Milly-Molly-Mandy* books or the *Amelia Ann* or even the Clifford Webb books with their lovely pictures and well and simply told stories.

The degree in which a child appreciates the impossible

and in fact demands, in his stories, situations and behaviour which would not occur in reality seem to be in proportion as he himself is able to distinguish between reality and imagination. The clearer he is about this distinction the more he enjoys and relishes at its full value the 'make-believe' of the story; that is why five-year-olds want more unreal stories than the four-year-old. But within the limits of fantasy certain rules of logic, reason and behaviour must be adhered to, exactly as for the younger children. Although the characters may do things, and events may occur, which in the real world would be impossible, standards and values of behaviour and ethics must be those of the child's real world.

Nursery rhymes and jingles are just as popular as with younger children; rhythm and rhyme have such an appeal that children will listen entranced to poetry they can hardly understand provided it has sufficient rhythm and jingle, and goes with a swing.

The beginnings of reading

Five-year-olds who have had stories read to them for one or two years have been showing an increasing interest in how the story appears in print. They enjoy looking at the book, apart from the illustrations; they know now many of their stories by heart and often pretend they are reading by telling the story and turning over the pages at the right moment! They ask which printed words say the part of the story they have repeated. They have become interested in the letters and words which are printed large on hoardings; they will even say: 'I want to learn to read.' This does not mean that the moment they have said this children are ready to do lessons every day, but it does mean that if we provide them with suitable material they will spasmodically concentrate on sorting, reading, tracing and even copying letters. They will also put letters together into words with great pleasure. They will learn the sounds of the letters if a grown-up will give them a good alphabet book in which each picture really does give the sound of the letter written by its side. Large wooden or plastic letters, a simple work-making or picture-naming game, all these are splendid ways of satisfying this newly awakened ambition.

It is the same with numbers. There are several number books and number-making games on the market which children enjoy playing with. All normal and healthy children can and do learn both their letters and numbers (at least up to 10) quite incidentally as they learn other things, without being 'taught', if the material is provided for them to do so.

MUSIC

As a baby grows and his speech develops his interest in music quickly changes from that of a passive and happy listener. He becomes an active participant in music making —noise, some parents call it! Rhythm is a most primitive human instinct, and rhythmic movement and noise make their appearance very early in the child's life. Drums, if the adult's nerves are sufficiently strong, are the best instruments to give to a small child. But they must be strong. Tin drums covered with paper or very thin vellum are bad —they burst easily and are also easily battered out of shape. The best are wooden-framed drums covered with thick vellum. Cymbals, bells and triangles are also good percussion instruments which children love.

By the age of three a small child who has had nursery rhymes sung to him since he was born, will know many of them if not word or sound perfect. The nursery rhymes which form such an important part of our national heritage

The Nursery Years

have that intrinsic quality about them which makes them seem to come almost naturally to a small child, and to remain unforgettably in the memory.

Between three and four the child will perfect his knowledge of these, practising the songs at all times of the day; there are, in particular, certain times of day and certain activities which seem to stimulate this need for song. One is on waking in the morning and going to sleep, another is bath-time, and yet another when playing with dolls. Nursery-school teachers who are tempted to have one fixed music period, and apart from that no singing, might well take this into consideration when planning their curriculum.

Percussion instruments are not melody makers, they are essentially rhythm makers. So young children, if they are not to be deprived of real music, should have the chance of hearing some instrument. A gramophone is a very useful present for any child over five years of age; it enables him to hear several instruments either separately or together. There are many gramophone records on the market of nursery rhymes, and other songs and dances for children, as well as music of our great composers which is simple enough to delight any child. If there is a piano at home a child should certainly be allowed to strum on it.

Chapter Three

THE DISCIPLINE OF THE NURSERY
YEARS

OUR RIGHTS AND THEIRS

THE third year brings the capacity for social life and naturally with it the necessity for social discipline. The tentative approaches which were made in the second year have led the child either to seek a closer acquaintance with other small humans because his mother has helped him, by her handling of each situation, to make the right approaches, or he shuns and attacks them alternately, if she has checked him violently or angrily in the past.

Not only is social discipline going to be required of him in regard to other children; his growing powers of action make discipline through indirect methods of distracting him from a harmful action, or the removal of everything he could damage, more and more difficult to carry out in practice. The time has come when his power of comprehension both of language and actions on the part of others makes it possible for the child to begin, however slightly, to understand reasoning. If we keep clearly in mind that discipline means in practice ability to live happily with others, enjoying our rights and allowing others theirs, we shall have gone far towards understanding the occasions

The Discipline of the Nursery Years

on which to help a little child in his adjustments. If, further, we try to see life from his standpoint we shall know much more about what he looks upon as his rights and consequently avoid disciplinary actions which can only be harmful to the child as well as most distressing to ourselves. For a little child's rights are often in opposition to ours; take for example his just need to get dirty and mother's right to save herself more washing than is absolutely necessary. Where our needs are in conflict the only fair way of dealing is to reach a compromise; furthermore, since adults understand so much more it is only fair for the compromise to be weighted more heavily in favour of the child. Yet how rarely does this happen? If mother meets a friend while she is taking small Jane for a walk, she will stand and talk until she has had enough without the slightest regard to Jane's interest which is to continue the walk. She may even get cross with Jane for fidgeting and interrupting the conversation.

The world from the child's point of view brings us at once to the relation of play to discipline. If we agree that young children, at least up to six, require the material which has already been described, and opportunity to use it properly, we have at least an understanding of some of the rights of the children and a basis for compromise when these rights conflict with those of the adults or with those of other children. Adults have memory and foresight; children have very little, for the present occupies all their attention. So it is up to us, knowing their needs, to plan daily life at home and abroad in such a way that the children get as much opportunity as possible to satisfy their needs, without its encroaching too much on ours. If we need a quiet hour during the day to do some work or to have a talk with a friend we will plan that time for the period when a small child is at rest or asleep. If there is no such time in the day then we arrange for an evening. If it is possible for the children to have a room of their own, then it is quite fair to expect them to have their messy play there and be tidy in the rest of the house.

How can we arrange for the small child to have his quota of experimenting, making messes, practising his skills without turning the house upside down? Fortunately young children are prepared to be reasonable if proposals are fair, and their needs are met. Even a two-year-old can be persuaded that water should not be poured all over the floor if he is given a bowl of water in the garden, or allowed to splash in the kitchen sink. Although he may protest when water play is stopped, his protest will not in fact last long if he has his quota of splashing regularly every day. If he is allowed to get really messy when he plays with paint or dough, or clay, he will usually be willing to be tidied up to go out, or greet visitors.

For the young children time does not exist. The present is all there is and it is an endless present. Adults plan their daily routines, and if they plan them wisely they take into consideration the children's specific requirements. Children who wake early and go to bed early need a different time-table from those who wake late and go to bed late. Whether or not a three- or four-year-old should have a rest during the day should depend not on the mother's wishes but on the child's need, which he will show quite clearly in his conduct. Since time does not exist for him, requests from grown-ups to change from one occupation to another, as, for instance, to leave off play to go to lunch, or for a walk, always come as a shock. Besides giving children adequate reasons for the change, we can help them to accept it by warning them beforehand. That goes a long way to prevent a clash of interests.

Children begin to learn nature's stern discipline from

the day they are born. No amount of crying or stamping will prevent fire from burning them if they get too near it. They have to learn the discipline of skills at whatever occupation they take up. A tantrum will not prevent the paint from trickling down the sheet of paper pinned on the wall; only skill in finding out the right quantity of paint to use. Nature's lesson is not an easy one to learn, but children do learn it because they find they need it in order to achieve success in what they do. If human beings were as consistent and as patient as nature in applying social laws and the social laws were as self-evident as those of nature there would hardly be any disciplinary problems at all! The key to success in the discipline of daily routine is that the demands made on the child should be the least that are required for health, protection from danger, and the needs of others. On the other hand, a deman once it is made, should appear to the child as absolute as the need to lift a foot to climb a stair and the consequences of an action to be as logical and inevitable as that of putting your hand in the fire. When a cup has been emptied on to the floor, the mess must be cleared up. When walls have been scribbled over they must be washed clean again.

THE DISCIPLINE OF HOME ROUTINE

If then we accept the child's right and need to occupy himself daily with the kind of materials and equipment which have been described in the last chapter, discipline falls into place under the following headings:

1. How can these activities be fitted into the framework of a home, giving all the other members their share of space and time and enabling daily practical life to go on?

2. How can all the child's other needs, such as food, sleep, warmth, fresh air, etc., be provided for without

interfering with his need to play and be active and by making use of his willing co-operation?

3. Lastly, how can he be brought to accept the give and take of social life, the sacrifice of his own immediate interests in favour of those of others in return for goodwill and affection, the sharing of toys and activities, the willingness to conform to social rules in the interest of the whole group?

The answer to 1 and 3 is in fact that it is very difficult without a nursery school to help. It is almost impossible for one home to provide all that is required for healthy and full development. The companionship of other children younger, older, and of the same age, is also essential for full mental as well as social development. The importance of the nursery school will be discussed in the next chapter.

In the meantime home can, of course, provide a good deal of what a little child needs, and can bring in small friends as well as any brothers or sisters who may be there already.

There are a few simples rules about young children and their adaptability which have proved to be true in practice. One is that a happy contented child is always more willing to conform to an adult's request than an unhappy one.

Another is that a child is more likely to agree to do, or cease doing, something for which he is given a reasonable (to him) explanation. We often forget, perhaps we may completely fail to know, that children in their nursery years have little understanding of cause and effect, of consequences which may follow an action, of how most natural laws operate. This ignorance often leads them to do damage quite unwittingly. A four-year-old girl once dropped a cup she was carrying; it broke as it fell on the floor. Her mother rebuked her for 'breaking' the cup. The little girl was most indignant and answered, 'I didn't break it—I only let it go and it breaked itself.' This was quite true. When small children spill or break things they usually burst into tears, and it may take a long time to comfort them. This is because they had not foreseen the accident and are terribly surprised and upset at what has happened. We must help them to learn as quickly as possible.

A third simple rule is that children learn very quickly from example. Parents who hit and slap or shake, who shout or are rude, who are angry and swear, cannot be really surprised when their young offspring reproduce their own behaviour. A little child who is smacked for doing something his mother objects to will quite naturally turn around and do exactly the same thing to her.

Young children, because of their own ignorance and helplessness tend to look upon adults as all powerful, all-knowing and, generally speaking, perfect. The disillusionment comes gradually as the children themselves become more experienced and knowledgeable. If only parents, and teachers too, could remember that their actions, their words, their attitudes and feelings towards things and people are closely followed and observed by the children who quite naturally take them all as an example and standard for their own behaviour! Perhaps they would consider their behaviour objectively from time to time and ponder whether it does set the children a good example! The fact that the children do not succeed in being just what their parents are, or doing what their parents do, does not prevent them from wanting to be like their parents and from taking their behaviour in all things as the example of all that is perfect.

The Discipline of the Nursery Years

These simple rules should show us the way in which a child can be brought to understand why his conduct is right or wrong, and if wrong to be willing to modify it in the right direction. One of the things which makes for serious difficulty between adults and young children is the difference between their needs which are often in conflict; then the adult's needs are taken for granted, such as the need for peace and quiet, orderliness, grown-up conversations, cleanliness, but the children's are held to be unimportant and consequently to be set aside if they interfere with the adults' requirements.

The child's needs for his own activities are just as vital for his healthy growth as ours are for our peace of mind. There are two excellent maxims for daily life in the house. One is, 'Let Johnnie get on with his play if it hurts no one and does no serious damage to property'; the other is, 'plan the time and space in such a way that conflicting needs will not clash.' For instance, children must make a mess with such things as paint, clay, sand, dough, water. Organize these activities so that they cause the least amount of trouble and see to it that the children wear overalls or rubber aprons. When grown-ups and children get together the children quite reasonably clamour to be heard. Let the conversation be theirs; the adults will have all the evening to talk quietly together when the children are in bed.

Because they desire so much to be grown up, children naturally wish to do all the things adults do in the house; that, for them, is the symbol of adulthood. They will do the things whether you allow them or not. If you forbid them, they will do them when you are not around to control the mess and disorder which will result. So you will, in the long run, have more trouble than if you patiently accepted the eager offer of help and put up with the inconvenience at the time you were going the job yourself. If a child is allowed to help with the washing, cooking, cleaning, sweeping, etc., it is far less likely to try its hand when you are not looking. It will also learn far more quickly how things are done properly and be less likely to cause damage whether wittingly or unwittingly.

If children are allowed a quota of noise, at certain times, in certain places, they are also more likely to accept being quiet at other times, to meet the requirements of the adults.

CARE, TIDINESS AND DAMAGE

The problems of care and tidiness in a home are nearly always sore points for both sides, the tidy and the untidy. The untidy suffer just as much from the tidy as the reverse. If adults cannot always agree about what constitutes a reasonable degree of tidiness, how shall we decide what is right for the children?

Most human beings are not tidy by nature. Many never become tidy at all; a few become obsessively tidy and spoil both their own lives and those of others. Obsessive tidiness may result from too much severity and too much nagging during the nursery years. Too much severity about tidying may also have the opposite effect.

If we are to live at peace with our neighbours and get on efficiently with our jobs, a certain degree of tidiness is essential. Systematic training from early youth does help to some extent, though it is not 100 per cent effective, as believers in habit formations would have us think. Children learn by experience, and are a very logical and reasonable race. If you give them good reasons for putting things away, it goes a long way to helping them to achieve this virtue.

The Discipline of the Nursery Years

A golden rule is that which says, 'always put one thing away before using another.' If we are consistent in applying this rule, and give tactful help on occasions, we will find children comply willingly enough.

In my nursery school this rule was accepted almost as a natural function, like dinner or rest: of course, the children had to be reminded. But then who hasn't?

This tidiness business is another reason against too many toys. It is easy to pull out toy after toy, to be distracted from one to another, and the resulting mess is so bad it is more than one child can tackle.

Another helpful hint to encourage tidiness is to give a child his own toy cupboard. It is valuable for a child to learn, by bitter experience if necessary, the logical reason for putting things away in their proper places and for keeping them in good condition.

Destructiveness is a characteristic which shows itself frequently in children, and it is easily aroused. That is one reason why toys should be made so as not to break easily. We want our children to learn to respect property which has cost man's labour to create. The best way to make young children appreciate the value of things is to set them a good example. If they see us caring for their toys and looking after them properly they will learn to imitate us. We can also forestall damage, on many occasions, and this should usually be done. There are times, however, when it is right for children to experience the consequences of their acts. When toys have been spoilt or broken they should immediately be removed; broken or damaged toys act as an incentive to destructiveness, and their continued use leads children to treat them with less care and respect. When a toy has been deliberately broken at home it is sometimes wise, when it has been removed, not to repair it for some days. The owner can then learn by experience that when a toy is broken it cannot be played with. In a nursery school, however, this should never be done, since many others besides the culprit would have to suffer. The children do mind, very much, losing toys, even for the few days which may be needed for the repairs. That is quite sufficient punishment in itself.

It is easy to lose toys, particularly small parts such as little pegs, cylinders, and bits of puzzles; all young children need adult help to prevent losses. The younger the child the less responsible he is and the greater help he needs. If an older child is very careless with his toys and loses them he should be left without their being replaced for a short time.

The older the child, naturally the more we can expect in the way of care, maintenance, tidiness and respect. The more a child is encouraged and helped to make things himself the more he will respect things made by others. Particularly in this sphere is example from adults contagious. In a home where there is a reasonable amount of tidiness and parents try not to nag, children will be more willing to put things away when they are bidden to do so. Having a room of your own is also very conducive to tidiness, at least tidiness in the grown-up's part of the house!

Children who are overloaded with toys at any age tend to become careless with them. It is not only that, having so many, it is more difficult to keep them tidy, but the very fact of having so many makes 'toys' cheap and valueless in a child's eyes. The children feel that if one were to get damaged it would soon be replaced, so it would not matter. As soon as children are old enough to understand that toys, like other useful articles made by man, cost human labour, they should learn to respect them for that reason. When, therefore, toys are broken or lost deliberately by older children, whose property they are, they should not be replaced. If the toys are repairable the children should be encouraged to do the repairs themselves. If, however, children lose or damage toys belonging to others they should be made to replace them by providing the money out of their own pocket money or savings, or by mending them, if this is possible.

These rules of conduct should, of course, apply to other things besides toys. Every article in a home has a use, and children must learn to know their uses and respect them. This learning takes time and adults must have patience and common sense. But, when children are old enough to know how to treat the material objects in their own small world, adults should not allow them to misuse these. Respect for things made by man is a very important part of social living.

THE DAILY ROUTINE

The most obvious thing about a daily routine time-table is that it should be suitable for the things you want to do. We plan our day so that all our work and play can be successfully carried out.

Children are at a very great disadvantage in this respect. They cannot plan their day because they are too young to be conscious of the future. At no moment can they say, 'I shall do so and so later on.' They only live in the present action, and what they do at any one time will, to a large extent, determine what they will do the next moment. So the grown-ups plan their day for them and on this planning will depend the child's willingness to conform to the time-table. If the plan takes into consideration the particular child's needs for his different activities, his food, his sleep, there is less chance of friction than if the plan is based on the assumption that all little children require twelve hours' sleep at night—one hour during the day—one heaped tablespoonful of green vegetables and so on. Nor can a little child's time-table be planned to the exclusion of other members of the family. But within the framework of any given family life the nursery child's needs can be well or badly met. If a child is an early waker it is useless trying to make him lie still in a cot until the family getting-up time. If he is allowed his toys he may be willing to play in his bed. It may, however, be necessary to let him get up. If the room is warmed in the winter and he has a warm dressing-gown he can come to no harm and the rest of the family will be able to rest in peace. If one child's early waking wakes another child who normally will sleep late, then try to arrange for them not to sleep together.

It is quite useless trying to make a nursery child sleep, or even rest, during the day if he strenuously objects. Some children need far more day-time rest than others. I have known babies who have given up sleeping at all during the day as early as eighteen months. My own child slept every day for at least one hour until she was nearly five years old. Some children need a heavy sleep during the day and then need to be put to bed later in the evening. If parents try to alter their child's rhythm for their own convenience they usually pay for it later by having a very disturbed child. Many children may protest at the actual time of being put into bed, but they will settle very quickly if they do in fact need sleep, and parents will discover this quickly enough. Twins I know of fifteen months protest loudly when they are laid down in their cots, but as they are usually tired their protests end abruptly as sleep overcomes them a minute or two after they have been put down.

MEALS

A healthy child has a healthy appetite. Three meals a day is the right number and the only thing which need be kept in mind, in order to ensure willingness to come to a meal, is that children, having no sense of time, should be warned beforehand that a meal-time is coming so that they can adjust themselves and get ready. When a child becomes 'negative' about meals in general there is certainly something wrong with the grown-ups' handling of this situation. Occasionally contrariness is best dealt with by allowing the child to go without his meal if he so wishes.

To stress good table manners when a child is still finding it difficult to handle a spoon, knife or fork and still finds 'playing' with his food a great delight, is to court disaster. If he is rebuked and made to eat in a way he finds too difficult he will turn against food and against meal-times.

OUTINGS

Children who are allowed to romp, climb, paddle in puddles and in paddling pools, play in sand and dabble in streams do not have to be coaxed or threatened into going out for a walk. At least, not if the walk means in a not too formally laid-out park or in the country. A walk round a block of flats, down a few streets, shopping or sitting on a bench are no use at all for anyone over eighteen months. Shopping will *have* to be done and may have to be done with the child or children; but if mother remembers that it is not the children's idea of an outing she will be patient with them, do the shopping as quickly as possible and give as much time as possible to the park. If there is a garden children do not need to be taken for walks at all during the summer months, unless they want to go. Play in the garden with garden toys, sticks, stones, old boxes, rugs, dressing-up clothes, bats, balls, sand and water, is usually more absorbing than walks in the summer. In the winter it is different. It is not easy to keep warm out-of-doors unless you are moving quickly all the time. Winter clothes hamper movement for play with toys, and anyway, apart from balls and skipping ropes, toys mean less running about than going for a walk. Because it is less attractive out-of-doors winter outings must be more tactfully arranged than summer ones. It is foolish to allow a little child to settle down to play with his toys and then call him out for a walk before he has had time to get tired of his play. It is best to plan outings either just after a meal or a rest. If, for instance, a mother has to do some shopping in the morning and has to take a small child with her, then it is best to go either immediately after breakfast, or if this is impossible, after the child has had a long playtime and is likely to be willing to got out because he is ready for a change.

TANTRUMS

Tantrums begin to appear usually in the second year. In the first year of life the baby's interest in anything he is doing is fleeting; his knowledge is too limited for him to have reached the stage of achieving an end or even wanting to achieve an end. So he is never disappointed. When something is being done to him which he dislikes, such as being washed (as opposed to being bathed) or having his diaper changed, or being dressed, he simply cries his protest either until the unpleasant action is over or his attention has been successfully distracted by mother or nurse. He has not yet come seriously against the laws of nature in his investigation of the world.

With the second year things change very significantly. Long hours of waking life have given him an opportunity to begin learning, with ears, eyes and hands. Locomotion is a key factor in development. Once he can walk and negotiate obstacles in his way, move objects about, see these being used for different purposes by the adults and begin using them himself, even if in a very simple way, he is forced to find out the rules by which different things work. He will frequently fail to do the right thing and he will, in consequence, feel extremely frustrated. J. at fifteen months had often seen the nursery school children sliding down the slide, and was very found of standing at the bottom and watching them. She could not yet understand that you had to go round the slide, and up the ladder at the other end in order to come down. So she started walking up the slide itself; three times she started up, and of course slid backwards. After the third attempt she sat at the bottom howling and hitting the slide with her hands as hard as she could. When she had been sufficiently comforted she was persuaded to walk around the slide, helped up the ladder and learnt to slide properly. Many times in the day the toddler will fail to do what he wants. Steps he tries to climb, objects he wants to put away or take out, bricks he wants to balance, they all seem to him to do the wrong thing, and he gets furious. His fury is the fury of impotence at things he does not understand and it vents itself in screaming and hitting; sometimes the child throws himself on the ground and thrashes out with arms and legs. He needs adult help over this stage of his life. In the first place he needs comfort and reassurance over his failure to deal with the world, and in the second he wants to be helped to overcome his difficulties and be successful in whatever it was he was trying to do. Every time a baby is able to overcome a difficulty he has gained in knowledge and ability. More important still, he has gained assurance and confidence which will help him to face new problems.

There is also another occasion which may lead to a tantrum. However careful the adults may be in organizing the environment of the toddler, there is certain to be quite a number of objects he may not touch or things he may not do. You will try to distract his attention to something else when you remove the object from him or stop his action, but this may not succeed. He will kick and scream. There is nothing to do except to wait patiently until the attack is over. Sometimes it is best, and necessary, to hold the child gently, but firmly. When the screaming stops the baby is usually exhausted, shivering and sobbing. He needs to be comforted and quietened. By that time he will almost certainly have forgotten what the fuss was about and will be ready to start life again if the grown-up will help.

Most children have learnt to control the tendency to give way to a tantrum by the time they are four, particularly if the grown-ups have helped them in the early years. But, at whatever age a tantrum is used, the method of handling it remains the same.

NEGATIVE BEHAVIOUR, RUDENESS AND BAD LANGUAGE

Almost all small children go through a stage of marked deliberate 'negativism'. Whatever you ask them to do, they do just the opposite. This stage begins when a baby realizes his own separate personality and understands the language his mother uses. Until he can walk moderately well language has accompanied his joint movement with an adult, as when he is picked up, dressed, and taken about to do all the things he does during the day. Words have been an accompaniment to his own actions or part of a total action or game. When he can move about separately from others and his mother says, 'Come here', he begins by doing so; it is part of the game of walking. Then he discovers, to his amazement, that he is now able to move, not only separately from her, but in any direction he likes. Doing the opposite of what he is told *is*, for the toddler, simply his way of asserting (for himself as much as for others), that he can think and choose for himself. This stage rarely lasts for more than a year, usually less. The simplest way of getting co-operation from the baby is to give the opposite order from the one you really wish to give! Alternatively, it is wise sometimes to avoid giving an order and use other methods to gain the same end. Very often the negative behaviour on the child's part is for fun and after a minute or two of asserting his right to be contrary he calmly changes and does as he is bidden. Real, deliberate negative behaviour begins later on. It has at its roots exactly the same motives as rudeness and bad language. All these aspects of behaviour, if they appear frequently, are almost always either attempts to gain attention because the child feels neglected or to revenge himself on the adult world because he has a grievance.

All children are negative, rude and ill spoken on occasions; life cannot be a continuous pleasure and many things have to be done which children dislike doing, like washing, or stopping their play for bed, and children often fail in what they are trying to do.

When a child refuses to do something which must be done the best way is to let him suffer the consequences of his refusal, but not to become annoyed. If he will not get dressed in the morning he will not have his breakfast, since he cannot come to the table undressed. If the adults only require children to do things which are really essential for their welfare and not unnecessary and foolish, then it is really always possible to make the children experience consequences which are not pleasant and which they can understand. If, however, after reasoning and explanations have failed, and a natural consequence is difficult to find, a child may have to be made to do something, such as get a coat on to go out because mother must get the shopping done, it should be done quickly and without anger. The fact that the child has had to be dressed against his will is sufficient 'punishment'; he should be helped by the adult to forget his negativism and take an interest in what is going to happen next. On no account should a child be made to feel he is rejected, unloved and bad because his behaviour at any moment may be wrong. He can be told his present behaviour is bad, but not he himself. A child, over three at least, is quite capable of understanding the difference between himself at any given moment and himself in general.

Rudeness and bad language usually begin to appear at about four years. Generally speaking they take the place of hitting, biting, scratching, pulling hair and so on. That is to say, they show a step in advance in the control of bad feeling arising out of some kind of frustration of personal wishes and actions. Suppose it is time to clear toys away and in spite of an early warning and offer of help from the grown-up the child still objects to stopping his play. At two or three he may turn on the adult and hit or bite if he does not throw a tantrum. At four or five he will probably control himself physically and give vent to his feelings by using bad words or being rude. He will probably say, 'I hate you, I will kill you, I will chop you into little pieces, I will run away from you and you will never see me again.' All this is far preferable to physical force. If his remarks are accepted as something he cannot help because he feels so badly, and are ignored, the child will gradually outgrow the habit because he finds it never has any effect and, in particular, never prevents the thing being done (or undone, as the case may be) which his words were meant to stop. Above all, the grown-ups must show the children, in their own practice, that rudeness is something the adults never have recourse to. It is at this stage, when the power of speech is just being understood, that children look upon it as a kind of magic. What is said is always taken as true, however absurd it may be. When one child says to another 'I will chop off your head', the latter bursts into tears and runs to the grown-up howling, 'Johnnie says he will chop off my head.' It takes a long time for children to fully realize that language, just as actions, can often be pure fantasy. Michael, a small boy of five, was once in a very bad mood at lunch-time. He teased and annoyed his neighbours at table and finally poured salt all over the plate of one of them. This was too much for the teacher, who firmly put him outside the room with his dinner and told him to eat alone since he could not eat sensibly with the other children. A minute later the door opened, Michael put his head round the door and shouted, 'I won't eat my dinner out here.' The teacher replied quite quietly that it did not matter if he ate it or not, he could do as he pleased about that. The door closed once more and reopened again a moment later, and Michael shouted, 'If I don't eat my dinner I shall die and then you'll be sorry.' He then burst into tears. The teacher reassured him and said nobody died from missing a meal. Michael retreated without tears, ate his dinner and returned to have his sweet with the other children.

The use of swear words and obscenities, apart from pure repetition of words which the children have heard and use quite innocently, without any understanding or ulterior motive, fulfills the same purpose as negativism or rudeness when these are used to gain attention. It is a true, but sad, fact that it is much easier to overlook the 'good' child who is busy playing sensibly than the naughty child who constantly draws attention to himself. Showing off in public or when out on a visit to friends or relatives has the same origin. Parents, whose children show much of this kind of behaviour should ask themselves whether they are giving their children the attention, interest and care which they should have. All children *feel* rejected and neglected when a new baby arrives in a family, even though in practice they are not. It is quite natural to feel in this way for small children's affections are, generally speaking, exclusive. While they love their mothers very strongly they care less for their fathers. When they develop a passion for these they cool off towards their mothers. Children want brothers and sisters, but this does not prevent them from being jealous as well. Parents need to be very forebearing with the older children, during the new baby's first six or twelve months, and give them extra attention, extra love and sympathy. They must accept returns to babyish ways, such as a desire to be dressed and fed although the children can well dress and feed themselves, to sit on mummy's lap far more than they did previously, to be unable to walk and need to ride in the pram and so on. This phase does not usually last more than a month or two if mother accepts it without comment. It is at this time that children may begin using bad language, showing off, and generally making themselves a nuisance, because their noses are out of joint. If little attention is paid to the bad behaviour and the children get the extra attention they need because of the baby, the phase will soon pass off.

There is another reason besides neglect which will lead to rudeness, bad language, negativism and so on. That is when the child feels that he is a failure or that life is a miserable affair instead of a happy venture. That a young child should feel this way at all is a direct reflection on the way in which his parents have treated him. A baby sets out on his journey at birth just as ready to find life good as to find it bad. No child is born bad-tempered, selfish, or cruel any more than kind, gentle and considerate. They develop these characteristics in the process of growing up as their response to the way in which the world treats them. If the grown-up world puts too many obstacles in their way in the form of 'tabus' on activities to which the children have a right, because they are the means of learning and developing, such as getting messy with water, clay or mud, or making a noise or deprive them of the materials for the kind of play which has been discussed, then the children will turn to occupations which are not allowed and they will become naughty children, whose response to the adults' rebukes and punishments is 'bad behaviour'.

There is, however, the opposite treatment of young children which, curiously enough, leads to the same kind of bad behaviour when the children have to face the outside world, in the form of either other children or school. That is parents who allow children to indulge their individual wishes and actions without regard to the needs of others or the community as a whole. Parents who give the children no help in controlling their feelings and their actions and even prevent them from experiencing the consequence of their actions, as for instance, replacing a toy which has been deliberately broken in a fit of temper; who allow anti-social behaviour both at home and in public either because they think it wrong to repress the children in any way or because they cannot face the task of dealing with the children in their struggle to become civilized. Giving children every opportunity to satisfy their needs and exercise their skill and faculties is only half of the parent's task. The other half, more exacting and difficult, is to help the children to face and overcome the difficulties of life and to control and socialize their egotistical tendencies. This requires active help from the parents as well as a great deal of love and patience.

Chapter Four

THE SOCIAL LIFE OF THE NURSERY

THE BABY'S FIRST CONTACTS

THE child's awareness of himself as a being distinct from others and his realization of their separate identity has for the first time brought him to the possibility of conscious and voluntary contact and association with others. Naturally this does not appear overnight. It has been developing slowly throughout the second year. A baby should be given the opportunity of meeting other babies from the time he is able to walk. Most babies have such opportunity, for mothers meet with their offspring in the parks, playgrounds and also at the Welfare Centres.

These first contacts with other small humans are extremely important, because on them, to a very large extent, will depend the child's attitude to other children when he begins to attend nursery school. A child's first relationship with other human beings is with adults, or perhaps with other brothers and sisters; it has never been a meeting of equals. He has investigated these older people to his heart's content whenever they have been within reach of his hands, just as he has investigated anything else. When he has scratched, clawed, pinched or bitten too hard he has been gently stopped or moved out of clutching distance. His unwitting unkindness has never been met with cries or screams. But things are quite different when he tries to investigate another baby. It is therefore important for mothers to guide and help their children in these first approaches to social contact if the children are to find pleasure in each other's company instead of displeasure. As the babies do not know what they are doing, to slap or scold them for hurting each other would be worse than senseless. They must be shown how to handle each other, what acts are 'right', which are 'wrong'. They can only learn this through experience, frequent experience, with the kindly help and guidance of the grown-ups. It is this experience, good or bad as it becomes, according to the adult's handling of each situation, which will determine the child's capacity to accept the discipline of social play, which increasingly becomes his most important means of growing into a social member of a community.

If screams and tears on one or both sides, result from experimental pushes, bites, scratches, caresses, hair pulls, offers of gifts and the hundred and one other overtures which small babies make to each other, and the adults either do not interfere at all, or slap and scold if they do, then the children begin to feel afraid and anxious. The experience is similar to one of failure in dealing with some practical activity. The babies do not know what went wrong, and then, do not know how to change their behaviour. So they either withdraw to a safe solitude or become aggressive with the intention of ridding themselves of the cause of their trouble. On the other hand if the adults help the children by showing them what to do with each other the children gain confidence and begin slowly to establish a working partnership with each other. One of the first social games to appear is that of 'I give it you and you give back to me, quick.' It works very well with the grow-ups, because they will respond. It doesn't work so well with other babies because they naturally will not always respond. But here again if the adults interfere judiciously things go all right.

The small child who has had other babies of his age to play with from time to time with understanding and sympathetic adults about, tends to be more active, more independent, lively and happy than one who hasn't. Companionship even from the second year seems to have a very stimulating effect on development generally.

THE TWO-YEAR-OLD NEEDS COMPANIONS

Certainly by two years of age a child is beginning to require regular daily companionship. It is the expression of this interest in other babies which begins to make his mother think that he should play at least part of each day with other children. Furthermore, if we stop to consider the wealth of equipment which children between two and six years of age should have for their best development, we realize how essential a nursery school is. It is one of the tragedies of our times that the hope of more nursery schools, which the wartime day nurseries awakened, has not been fulfilled. The wartime nursery, in spite of many shortcomings, did, by its very existence, bring very forcefully to the public knowledge the need of the young child between two and five years of age, for nursery school life. The purpose of this chapter is to explain in what manner the nursery school provides for the child's needs and how it is a corollary of the home, not a substitute for it, for it provides for those needs which the home, even the best, cannot, in the nature of things, supply for the child from the time he is over two years of age.

When discussing a nursery school we naturally take as

The Social Life of the Nursery

our standard the best school in the country, and base our requirements on the most up-to-date study of the child's needs—physical, emotional, intellectual and social.

A nursery school teacher has two very great advantages over a mother. In the first place she has premises which are planned and arranged specifically and exclusively for the use of children between the ages of two and five years. In the second place she herself has only one job to do, and that is to look after the children.

A mother has to 'mind' the child while she does her housework or cooking. So long as the baby cannot get about it is fairly easy for the mother to do her housekeeping and give the child all the attention he needs. But once he is able to move about easily on two feet the situation changes very considerably.

It is one thing to handle a child when all your attention can be given to the task, and quite another when it is just an extra piece of work on top of many other things which must be done and thought about.

When young R. deluged the classroom by filling a watering can at the tap and pouring it over himself, he triumphantly showed the watery floor to the teacher when she returned. 'Look,' he said, 'it all goes on the floor!' She was neither worried nor flurried, for it didn't really matter if he and the floor got wet, and there was plenty of time to change and learn to mop the water up.

But it was quite a different matter when J., at the age of eighteen months, got hold of some blacking in the kitchen and succeeded in covering herself, the table legs, and a large portion of the floor with it. It was no joke at all, because, having the dinner to cook, her mother had to clean her up as quickly as possible and put her somewhere where she could not get into mischief again.

If your mind is not occupied with any other immediate

task it is much easier to give a child the right attention, to remain patient in the face of exasperating behaviour on the part of the child, and to give encouragement and help when they are required. It is also much easier to refrain from helping in order to get something done; for it is naturally difficult for a mother who must go out to do the shopping to wait patiently for a quarter of an hour while small John tries to do up his leggings. But in a nursery school the only important things are the leggings.

This difference is, I think, very often overlooked by teachers, who forget the advantage of having nothing but the children to think of.

Then there is the special environment of the nursery school which counts so much in adapting the child's every-day life to his needs. Children who attend a nursery school develop both physically and mentally far more rapidly than those who do not; for not only is all the play material provided carefully selected with this aim in view, but everything in the environment, such as wash basins, w.c's, hooks, and lockers, is so arranged that small children can carry out their daily activities with the minimum of assistance. There is nothing more conducive to developing confidence and ability to act in a small child than the knowledge that he can perform daily tasks, such as washing himself, dressing, turning taps on and off, laying his own dinner table, etc., without adult aid.

The nursery school teacher has an ideal setting for her work in this respect, and there is literally no limit to the freedom she should give to a small boy or girl learning to handle the tools which serve these activities.

But perhaps the most important aspect of the nursery school lies in its social life. It enables a two-year-old to adapt himself to other children of his own age. The importance of this cannot, I think, be overestimated. For this

adjustment is difficult, and the older the child is before he
begins to make it the more difficult it is to make. Because
a two-year-old is still almost entirely an individualist it is
easier for him to adapt himself to a number of other little
individualists around him. They pay little attention to each
other, yet at the same time they learn to tolerate each other
and to play happily without interfering with the play of
others. They forget to be shy and self-conscious among
other children, and as the desire for co-operative play
begins to develop it finds its natural expression among the
companions the children have learnt to know and become
familiar with since they first came to school. They also
learn early to share their play material, to take turns on
such things as slides, swings and fun boats. They thus learn
quite naturally at an early age to curb their possessive
instinct before this has had time to develop very strongly.
A child who has remained an only child, or even a younger
or elder of two, till he is five or six years old, finds it much
harder to learn to share at that age than he would have
done at two or three.

The daily social contact with other children of the same
age is as important a factor in helping to increase a child's
self-confidence and assurance as the equipment which
enables him to become independent of adult aid. Both are
major factors in helping forward his mental and physical
development.

Two very shy children came to my nursery school the
same term, one a boy of two and a half, the other a little
girl of five. Within three weeks the boy, who refused to
say a word to anyone, child or adult, the first week at
school, had quite forgotten to be shy and was as friendly
as any of the other children; but the five-year-old girl took
nearly a whole term to settle down and become really happy
and free among her companions.

The Social Life of the Nursery

For a two-year-old by far the most important activities in life are those connected with the actual process of living from day to day: that is, dressing, washing, eating, bathing, going to the lavatory, going out and coming in. These naturally include all the subsidiary activities connected with them, such as laying tables, turning on taps, washing up.

The nursery school therefore provides equipment and fixtures most suitable for the child to learn to look after himself unaided; it is also most important, in the nursery school routine, to give plenty of time and importance to all these activities. As much prominence and importance should be given to washing for dinner as to play-room occupations. The children should help as much as possible with such activities as getting out their rest beds, laying the tables, clearing up, etc. Not only do they enjoy doing these things, but the responsibility laid upon them promotes self-reliance and independence.

One of the most popular occupations in the nursery school is scrubbing the tables with soap and water after dinner. A four-year-old once put a great deal of elbow grease and soap into scrubbing his table and succeeded in covering it with thick soap suds. He was so pleased with the effect that he came into another room to fetch me to have a look at it. 'Look what a lovely lot of soap,' he said. 'I can make lines through it with my finger.'

If the children are to help in the daily tasks which need doing, it inevitably means allowing a mess to be made, and a well-run nursery school always allows this. There is also the equally important task of 'clearing the mess away'. A

94

little girl was shown how to wipe up the water she had spilt by mistake. She was so excited that she promptly spilled much more in order to be able to wipe it up.

It is perfectly natural to make a mess over certain activities, and it is just as natural and proper to clear it up afterwards.

Just as the fixtures and furniture of the nursery school are planned to enable the child to do a great deal for himself, so the teacher's attitude should be always to give as little assistance as is required to help the child keep confidence in himself and succeed in overcoming the difficulties in his way. A timid, nervous child will need more help and encouragement than a self-assured and capable one, but the stress should always be to encourage him to do things alone. In particular a child who is very independent and who rejects offers of help should not have it forced upon him, even if it means that he will not succeed in what he is trying to do.

Next in importance to learning to look after himself unaided, for a two-year-old, are all the things adults do and which he wants to be able to do himself. To satisfy this second need the nursery school should provide him with exactly the same implements, only to scale, which the adults need for all household activities. This, however, is not sufficient. Small children have naturally only a limited capacity for effort and concentration; they are also easily discouraged by failure. So that the amount of real housework, such as sweeping, dusting, washing, cleaning, which they can accomplish is relatively small, considerably smaller than the amount they wish to accomplish; moreover, there are certain tasks they cannot do at all, but which they nevertheless wish they could do. They will therefore satisfy these wishes in imagination; there is nothing harmful in this, provided, of course, that a child does not make this play a substitute for real achievement, seeking satisfaction only in imagination for something he refuses to undertake in reality.

It is therefore just as important to provide a nursery school with the tools for imaginary household and family activities, i.e. dolls' furniture, cups and saucers, pots and pans, as with the tools for the real work.

It is also in the sphere of imaginative play that co-operation between children occurs most frequently among children under six or seven, and it is very important for their social development.

The importance of group play among nursery school children cannot be overestimated. It is not simply that children lose their shyness, curb their possessive instincts, and learn to share, important as all these are.

GROUP PLAY

Group play lays the foundation of character development which will enable the children to become genuinely co-operative workers, capable of sensitive leadership, considerate and tolerant of the views, ideas and wishes of others. Above all it gradually makes them conscious of the pleasure and satisfaction which comes of being active members of a community. It is essentially this satisfaction which enables the children to sacrifice their own interests and possessions in favour of those of other children, to yield the leadership in a game and to work for others.

Spontaneous group play, usually centred round imaginative games, which begins round about the fourth year of life, but had its roots in the early contacts of babyhood, is in no way comparable to the organized games of later school days. The team spirit, with its accent on co-operative group activity in observing rules and regulations and the sinking of individuality in the team, is a characteristic of later childhood and adolescence, and not of early childhood. When young children, certainly under eight or nine, are organized by adults for team games it does not bring out a team spirit. On the contrary the children seem quite unable to accept rules imposed on them arbitrarily by the game (they look upon them as imposed by the adults) and tend to become quarrelsome and competitive in the worst sense. It seems that, at this stage of life, co-operative activity can only be achived through spontaneous and voluntary association in connection with games which the children have invented and planned themselves, whose rules are of their own making. When this occurs it is quite remarkable the degree of discipline the children show; they obey orders from a self-appointed or chosen leader in a way they would never do for an adult; they meekly give up their individual wishes. I once watched some four-year-olds playing mothers and fathers, with a two-year-old. The latter was told to lie still under a large blanket in the corner of the room, while the others went 'shoping'. After a few minutes a muffled voice squeaked: 'Can I get up now?' 'Of course not', the others answered promptly and severely. The request was repeated twice and twice refused. I then intervened, thinking the younger child was being bullied, and lifted the blanket. The two-year-old was most indignant with me for interfering with the game and assured me he was very happy, suffocating under the blanket. The children do not, of course, play perfectly happily all the time without any quarrelling, nor can they be left entirely alone when playing. They need the help and guidance of grown-up people. It is easier for a teacher to give this help because she is in a much more objective position with regard to the children than a mother is when her own children are playing with friends.

The Social Life of the Nursery

It is only through this spontaneous, self-directed play that children can achieved these qualities of good neighbourliness, and it takes them all their years of childhood up to their junior school life to do so. Not all the children's activities contribute equally to this co-operative play. Some are almost unsocial, such as painting, doing puzzles, carpentry, riding tricycles. Some, on the contrary, are almost entirely social, such as Wendy house and father and mother play. It is rare to find a child playing alone in the Wendy house in a nursery school. Another very social game is that with miniature motors, buses, tractors and other equipment for laying out towns, villages, networks of roads, etc. Another is the use to which children put boxes, planks and ladders out in the garden and play in the sand among children over four years of age. All the play which seems to stimulate sociability is naturally encouraged in a nursery school and the material for it is provided so that it is attractive and inviting. It is particularly in connection with group imaginative play that children show ingenuity and their ability to use material which we would consider junk. That is why it is important for the Wendy house to be equipped as richly as possible, not with expensive teasets, cooking stoves, wardrobes and walky-talky dolls, but with plenty of the odds and ends no longer required by mother. Flat lids of small tins make excellent plates, bakelite screw-on tops of bottles make lovely dolls' drinking mugs. Sample bottles of perfumes and wines which might turn up from somewhere are delightful. Old blankets are much in demand to make 'houses' with, both indoors and out of doors.

Dressing up is another activity which is essentially social. If two nursery school children go to the dressing-up box and start dressing themselves up, in a few minutes several others have joined them and group play acting is

The Social Life of the Nursery

well launched. In this case, just as with games, the situation is quite different from that in which a teacher is organizing a dramatic period. The fact that it is the childrens' own spontaneous choice and that the content of their dramatic play is of their invention is what gives this activity its quality, particularly as regards social co-operation. The dramatic work with a teacher certainly has its merits, very great ones, but they are not those of stimulating this co-operation. It is only in their own play-acting that children evince those characteristics of leadership, acceptance of leadership and general planning and organization of themselves and each other which is so valuable.

The quality of group play increases very considerably in the fifth and sixth years, but children who first come to school at four or five having had little, or no, experience of play with other children, have often to go through the earlier stages of contact with others, that is the individualistic approach of the two- or three-year-old, who takes heed only of his own needs and wishes and cannot yet recognize those of others. When such children first play with four and five-year-olds who have experience of playing with others it is often necessary for the teacher to help and guide both the newcomers and the others; for these, having learnt the give and take necessary for their stage of development are bewildered and often annoyed at what they take to be anti-social behaviour on the part of the new children.

EXPERIMENTING: LEARNING FROM OTHERS

Not only have the children learned by four or five to play tolerably happily and co-operatively together when they have had several years of experience, they have also learned a great deal from each other. As increasing speech

The Social Life of the Nursery

broadens their sphere of contact, children eagerly impart to each other all the new items of knowledge which they have each gained, either through their own personal experience, or from information given them by older children or adults.

Here again it is easy to underestimate this source of development, for it is a difficult one to assess at any given moment. You can tell, by giving a child a sum to do or a page to read, just how far he has progressed with his lessons. But his general knowledge and, even more particularly, his capacity for thinking logically and for tackling problems are far more difficult to estimate. Moreover, it is almost impossible to assert categorically that he has gained this knowledge or ability in this or that way. It is, however, well established that children who come to primary school from a nursery school in which they have had a rich environment, including a garden with plants and animals, are, on the whole, more knowledgeable and are better able to tackle problems of learning than those who have come straight from home.

This ability to learn from other children in the course of play activity is clearly shown in the third group of nursery age interests, namely, the curiosity about how things happen, the rules governing natural phenomena and the function of all objects of a child's environment. The child wishes to discover the why and wherefore of every object he sees. He wishes to know how everything works, and through finding out he develops his senses and his intelligence: it is here that each child bringing his quota of existing knowledge helps to build up the common pool. And here again there is a great difference between such second-hand knowledge and that offered by the teacher in a lesson. The reason for this lies in the fact that knowledge volunteered by one child in a group activity carries meaning

Va. Village. All and any kind of oddments of wood can be used for the layout of a village

Vb. Playacting. Little is needed to stimulate it and it is well rewarding

VI. Paddling Pool

and is vitally interesting because it concerns something which at that moment holds the attention of the whole group.

The nursery school utilizes this impulse to discover and the energy it generates to help forward this development of the children, by providing certain definite material which serves this end.

Independence is as important in connection with the use of this material as it is with learning to dress or wash unaided. Children should be encouraged to try things they have not tried before, to attempt something just a little more difficult; above all, they should be allowed the use of so-called dangerous tools, so that they can learn how dangerous they are and wherein lies their danger. Naturally I only refer here to such dangerous tools as scissors, hammers, saws, and needles, that is to say, tools which a child can handle successfully; tools, such as sharp cutting knives, chisels, dangerous chemicals, all of which he could not use successfully even if he tried, and with which he could do very serious harm, should naturally be kept out of the child's environment. Moreover, when allowing saws to be used this should always be done under the supervision of an adult; apart from the fact that they are more dangerous than hammers and scissors, children under six cannot use them successfully without help. There is nothing safer than a child with a dangerous tool if he knows all about it, for his natural caution helps his reason and knowledge. It is those who know nothing about these tools who are a danger to themselves and to others when they find them.

Children must be given the freedom and opportunity to make discoveries and to experiment with the things they find in their environment. Not only is this the best way of satisfying their curiosity about the world, but by far the best way for them to gain knowledge and experience. Now, not everything in a child's everyday environment is equally suited for this purpose, nor is it equally possible to make discoveries about all things; e.g., it is easier to find out properties of water than of electricity. It is the function of the nursery school teacher to provide that material which lends itself best to satisfying experimentation.

The best material, as we have already seen in the earlier part of the book, is that which nature provides in a solid concrete form, earth, water, sand, clay, and all living and growing organisms. These are mostly found out of doors, although it is also important to bring them indoors as well so that the children can carry out these satisfying activities even though it is too cold or wet to be out of doors.

The fourth group of activities which grows in importance as the child gets older is that connected with his need to create. The two-year-old is not yet creative; he is still too busy learning how to use his hands and feet and finding out the properties of the materials he handles; but the three-year-old has already discovered that he can 'make' things out of sand and clay, paint and earth. This discovery is one of the most important steps in his development, for through his creation he satisfies many urges, many impulses; he gains emotional stability and control and he gains enormously in self-confidence and assurance. It is for this reason also that these materials are vitally important.

A last group of activities which are essential for healthy growth is composed of those connected with physical development. The nursery school must provide the equipment necessary for good physical growth.

In this sphere also a child should be allowed to do 'dangerous' things such as climb ladders, trees or walls, and it is the responsibility of the teacher to see that the use of the material for these activities cannot lead the child into greater danger than is involved in the bumps resulting from a short fall; that is to say, no wall or ladder should be so high that a fall would be really dangerous. Many children need encouragement and suggestion to undertake new and dangerous feats, and the achievement of these feats increases their self-confidence and abilities considerably.

Chapter Five

A NURSERY SCHOOL DAY

THE DAY'S ROUTINE

For his physical as well as his emotional welfare and security a young child needs a regular daily routine in the same way as he needs to see his mother every day and the familiar objects of his environment always in their place, day after day. But this routine must only be a framework within which he can move and act freely and confidently; it must therefore be of the simplest kind and it must be elastic. Moreover, the routine must only apply to a certain quite specific number of activities. These are his hours of sleep, rest and meals. These are the only things which should be fixed and stable, and even they should be capable of being occasionally altered without the child suffering from it. For the nursery school, times of arrival in the morning and departure in the afternoon should also be fairly regular and dependable, although here again it should be possible for times to be altered according to circumstances without the child feeling unsettled by the change. Apart from these fairly fixed times the child needs to be quite free to occupy himself as he chooses. A nursery classroom should always be on the the ground floor with direct access to the garden, so that

A Nursery School Day

children can at any time of the day, morning or afternoon, occupy themselves in or out of doors, and the teachers be able to supervise them.

Children, like adults, will put effort and concentration into their work when they are fresh and full of energy. This will naturally be in the mornings rather than the afternoons. We shall therefore expect them to play most purposefully in the first part of the day and to make use of the material which requires the most effort and thought. Some children will want to settle down to some constructional or creative activity as soon as they arrive in the nursery; others will prefer to run about, shout, climb and generally get rid of the surplus energy they have stored up during their last night's sleep before they settle down to quieter and more thoughtful work. The nursery class routine should allow for this; it is therefore very important to have the garden always available.

Children should be free to choose any play material and to play individually or in groups, whichever they prefer. They need material with which they can work independently, and the only conditions we need to impose on the use of play material is that it is not damaged, lost or spoilt, and that it is put away when no longer required.

Certain kinds of play material require elaborate preparations. Painting, for instance, is one of these. Not only are several things required, paints, dishes, paint-brush, paper, but also water and a piece of oilcloth to put on the table, sometimes even a rubber apron. The collecting and arrangement of these things are just as important to a two-year-old as the actual painting, and frequently take much longer. Many children will spend ten minutes getting their outfit ready, two minutes actually painting, and nearly fifteen minutes washing and clearing away; all these activities are equally important from the point of view of the

child's development and consequently should be allowed
their full expression.

Younger children require more solid toys, such as trains,
trucks, dolls and prams, fitting toys and tricycles; older
children, four- and five-year-olds, need more constructional
and creative equipment such as scissors, paper, crayons,
needles, wool and canvas, constructional toys, Dinky toys
for creative and group play. For younger children concentrate less and tend to be almost continually on the move
and their noise, though it may be less in volume than when
the older ones are being noisy, is more constant. For these
reasons it is wisest to have separate rooms for the younger
and older nursery pupils, with the different kinds of equipment. The children, however, should be free to move
about in the two rooms as they please, for older ones may
need from time to time to return to play with the toys in
the little ones' room and the younger ones frequently enjoy
watching older ones and even trying their hands at occupations which are still beyond their capacity.

Small children require fresh fruit daily and as much
liquid to drink as possible; it is therefore a good plan to
give a fruit drink in a nursery school at about 10.30, or at
least one hour after the beginning of school. One hour's
concentrated activities is usually sufficient for two- and
three-year-olds, and the drink provides a good excuse for
putting things away and doing something else. Fruit-time
is, or should be, important, because the children carry the
jugs, they pour the drink out, they pass the cups and mugs;
these are serious and difficult tasks and are important
because they have a social character.

The period immediately following the mid-morning
drink is often found the most suitable time for singing and
dancing, because the children have put away their play
material and have already been brought naturally into one

A Nursery School Day

group for the drink. The music period need not always occur at this time, nor should there necessarily be only one period; a few, or even all, of the children may want to sing and dance at other times of the day and sometimes quite individually, as, for instance, when playing with a doll.

But a music period should be given every day in a nursery school, for it is one of the best means of helping small children to lose self-consciousness and diffidence and learn to express themselves fearlessly in movement; two- and three-year-olds will often refuse to take any part, so will new-comers, but they usually enjoy watching the others do rhythmic movements, dance, and sing, and, if they are not pressed or urged, will soon join in themselves when they become familiar with the songs and dances. Those who definitely take no interest in music should naturally be allowed to do other things instead.

While children should be free to run in and out of the garden it is important to see that all of them are out at least for an hour each morning, unless the weather is quite impossible. In the winter during the cold spells it may be necessary to fix the outdoor play-time; I think that on the whole it is best to have this in the late morning because it is likely to be warmer than during the early hours. The weather conditions on any one day should be the determining factor as to when the children should go out in the winter months. In the summer the children should spend the whole day out.

Lunch at 12.30. Here again ample time should be given to such important functions as washing, going to the toilet, laying tables. Rest or sleep, for from one to two hours, according to age or individual requirements, should always follow the midday lunch, which is a small child's heaviest meal.

A Nursery School Day

By the time a little girl or boy gets up from his after-dinner rest the most strenuous part of his day is over. He is no longer capable of continuous effort or concentration and will, if left to his own devices, choose a make-believe game which, while involving very little work or energy, yields a maximum of satisfaction if only in wish-fulfilment. Many children, particularly those who sleep after dinner, take a long time to wake fully and prefer to sit about looking on at the others for some time after they have got out of bed. If the weather is sufficiently fine it is best for the children to play in the garden after their rest.

Whatever the detailed plan of a nursery school day may be it is essential to remember that: (1) Daily jobs such as washing, dressing and undressing, and domestic work such as cleaning, sweeping, washing up, cooking, putting things away, are as important as play activities and should be given as prominent a place in the children's daily life. Making biscuits, cakes and sweets is quite within the capabilities of children under five, if they have help, and an occasional cooking afternoon is well worth the trouble of the organization and work involved. (2) Children should feel 'at home' in the nursery school; this implies that the school must be, in fact, very like home; it must have the essential properties of home and these include such important places as the kitchen, passages, w.c's., washrooms and garden; these rooms are almost as important to a small child as his playroom. He should feel that they are as much his as the playroom and be free to go in and out as he wishes and as he does at home.

NURSERY SCHOOL MATERIAL

The play material provided in the nursery school must satisfy those needs of the young children which have already been described.

A Nursery School Day

For creative and experimental work it is essential to have water, sand, clay and paints as well as building bricks, paper, scissors, pencils and chalks. If it is possible to have a large sink fitted in the nursery playroom with hot and cold water, this is ideal, for the children can then do a great deal of experimenting while the teacher has her eye on them. One wall of the playroom should be fitted with blackboarding; this should begin not less than 12 inches from the floor, and reach not higher than 4 feet. Indoor sand should be in a large raised sand-tray, preferably zinc-lined.

For modelling, I would recommend modelling clay as the best material for young children, even though it requires a great deal of attention and care; it must, of course, be kept neither too dry nor too wet, but when of the right consistency it is ideal, and the children can clean it away very easily. For painting, large brushes, large sheets of paper, and large paint dishes should always be used, the paints should be bright, but there should not be more than three or four colours, of which three should be the primary colours—red, blue, yellow. Sheets of bright-coloured paper are also essential for cutting out and pasting; ungummed paper should be used.

Even two-year-olds will try to use scissors, and they often succeed as well; they should certainly be allowed to try. They should also have pencils, paper, paste, paints and water at their disposal just as four- and five-year-olds do, even though they can produce nothing but scribble and messes and bits of half-torn paper. That is how they learn to use their hands so that later on they can acquire the necessary skill. All these activities should be carried out preferably early in the day when the children are fresh.

Large hollow building blocks are essential for all ages from two to five and there must be a very large number of them, for they will frequently be in use. Small ones are also important for imaginative play with trains, carts, and small animals, houses, trees, etc., for making zoos, villages and farms.

There should be a number of trains, carts, boats, lorries, barges and vans. The best ones are those which can be made up of different parts, or at least different sections which can be coupled and uncoupled; trucks should be hollow so that they can be loaded with different kinds of goods.

Plenty of small wooden animals, houses, trees will be combined with building bricks and trains to make up quite elaborate imaginative play, often involving good social co-operation between several children.

All wooden toys, large or small, must be very well made, very strong and very simple.

There should be a number of dolls, unbreakable and preferably home-made; very large and expensive ones are not desirable. Teddy bears are also needed, but no woolly animals. Dolls' beds and prams and a certain amount of dolls' furniture and domestic equipment, such as tea-sets, are needed to stimulate and help imaginative play; but there should not be too much material, nor should it be too elaborate. Children should be able to utilize all kinds of junk, old pots and pans, jars, lids, old spoons and cartons for this play; they should have a large store of this type of material to choose from. For this domestic and home play there is another kind of equipment which plays a very important role in the children's development. This is the collection of different things they collect themselves—stones, sticks, all kinds of seeds, flowers, grass, shells—all these are turned to a very good use in domestic play.

Teachers should remember this and encourage and facilitate this activity in children.

A Nursery School Day

Dressing-up clothes play a big role in this kind of play and it is just as important for children to have them in the nursery school as at home. In fact they are more necessary since 'play-acting' is a social activity. The material required is not elaborate and expensive costumes, but all the odds and ends and remnants of grown-up clothes; old-fashioned garments are particularly welcome. Bits of lace and ribbon, old ladies' caps, the remnants of a silk skirt are things small children love. The favourite quality of dressing-up clothes is brightness and even gaudiness; brightly-coloured garments with frills and laces are most popular. During the nursery years the children's chief desire is to pretend to be grown-up and therefore they want adult clothes and not fancy costumes such as are made for fancy-dress parties.

It is also a very good plan to keep a large cardboard or wooden box full of oddments in the nature of old cotton-reels and odd bits of 'constructional' toys, such as 'Pick-a-Bricks', 'Matador', 'Cliptico', etc. Three- and four-year-olds are not able to construct models out of the sets, but if they have the odd pieces they love fitting them together to 'make' things. X, aged three and a half, made a curious contraption out of bits belonging to four different sets; it looked like nothing except bits of stick stuck together, but it was proudly called an aeroplane and showed off to everyone as such.

There should also be fitting toys of all kinds, from the very simplest for two-year-olds, graded right through to the most complicated for four- to five-year-olds. I include in this category simple puzzles such as the Abbatt animal ones. There should be also beads in quantities, of all shapes and sizes and plenty of laces to string them on. Peg-boards —little wooden pegs which fit into a board full of small holes to match—are quite popular with the younger children, and with different coloured pegs the children often make patterns, selecting and grading their colours. Posting boxes should also be there for the younger children. But it must be remembered that play with puzzles, fitting toys, pegs, etc., will not occupy children for long, nor does it satisfy their more urgent impulses and creative needs.

Hammer pegs are important for the small children. The older ones, certainly the four- to five-year-olds, will need real nails and real hammers and saws, and should be provided with a small carpentry bench.

From four years onwards children need more advanced work and materials than the fitting toys, building blocks and peg boards which occupy them at two and three years. They have learnt sufficient skill with their hands in the use of tools to want to make things; they want to use such material as raffia, wool, needles, cardboard, and oddments to make models with; they also want to learn their letters and numbers. If the four-year-olds are in the same group as two- and three-year-olds the best plan is to give them a half-hour's 'work' period when the babies are out in the garden; this is possible after fruit juice if the teacher has an assistant who can take charge of the younger ones for that period.

For the four-year-olds must have relative quiet and peace in which to work; they must also have the undivided attention of the teacher. This period should not be too rigid; but should merely give the older children the opportunity of beginning 'big children's' work when they feel the desire for it. Large, wooden cut-out letters and numbers should be used, and counting rods; for sewing and wool-work only the easiest things should be attempted, and particularly those which will show a result quickly; coarse canvas to be sewn with rug wool and a very large needle, or two cardboard rings and thick wool to make a fluffy ball with. If a four-year-old cannot make and finish an object

A Nursery School Day

very quickly he will not only lose interest in it, but become discouraged from further attempts at that kind of work.

Story reading is important for four-year-olds, and sometimes the brighter three-year-olds enjoy a story also. Story reading should therefore also come at a time when the smallest ones are out of the way and will not interrupt. The best kinds of books has already been described in the previous chapters. When reading to a group it will be found that the children frequently interrupt. These interruptions should not be stopped, because they are not a sign of lack of interest; on the contrary they show that the children are very interested. The interruptions may be due to three different causes; either the children want further explanation, or they wish to express their own feelings about the story, or, more frequently, the story has stimulated them to express themselves verbally. This stimulation to conversation is a very good thing, for it is but another way of forwarding development, both mental and emotional. I wonder how many teachers have observed that children who frequently cannot find a word to say on command during a 'daily news' period have all kinds of interesting things to say at story-time when they are told to be quiet?

Children, also, are very fond of hearing stories they know almost by heart—they will often take up the thread of the story when the teacher pauses and continue it themselves. This is excellent language and memory practise.

For music periods it is best to have a selection of percussion instruments—drums, cymbals, triangles, etc., all of which are useful for marking rhythm and time. A daily music period of ten to fifteen minutes is better for young children than longer periods twice or three times a week, because any activity which is part of their daily routine is more easily accepted and enjoyed as part of their everyday life. The music period should not be too rigidly fixed and percussion instruments should not be kept only for this work. The children should be free to use them in any of their games.

Picture books play an important part in early education; children of two and three years who do not care for story reading will nevertheless love looking at a picture book, and as they eagerly name all familiar objects which they recognize this occupation is excellent language practice. The most suitable picture books have already been described in previous chapters.

It is important to remember, when first equipping a nursery school: (*a*) the kind of material which is most necessary to all children and that which is least needed; (*b*) the play material which will be required in quantity and that of which only a little will be required.

The most important play material falls into two main groups:

(1) That required for creative, constructive and experimental play.

(2) That required for imaginative play.

For imaginative play we have to provide:

(i) Dolls, and all materials for dolls and domestic play; this includes improvised material such as tins, bottles, jars, cartons.

(ii) Prams, carts, trolleys, trains and all push-about toys. They must be strong enough to bear the weight of a child.

(iii) Building blocks.

(iv) Small wooden or lead animals, houses, trees, cars, etc., for farmyard, village or zoo play.

(v) Dressing-up clothes.

Different quantities will be required of these five different kinds; all the children will need dolls, building blocks, and pull-about toys, consequently more will be needed of these than of other things. The small children will require

A Nursery School Day

relatively little addition to a doll in the way of clothes and domestic equipment. Small wooden or lead animals and dolls'-house material will be needed chiefly for the four-year-olds, but they will want quite a good deal. This material can well be added to continuously. Building blocks you can never have too many of; both large hollow ones and small solid ones are needed, but more of the former. Since only the raw material, so to speak, is required for experimental and creative play, it is very easy to provide enough for a nursery class. But we must not forget that it is not sufficient to provide just bare water or bare sand; the children must have the tools to experiment with, and it is these tools which we must supply in quantity and variety; here again everyday articles are the best, old tins perforated with holes in different places, corks, spoons, funnels, rubber tubes, etc.

A sand-pit must be large; a square shape is the most use-ful. Sand and water trays must be large enough for at least six children to be able to play together.

A carpenter's bench and a few tools are sufficient since only the four-year-olds will work at this, and, as they need a good deal of help, it would not be practicable to have too many hammering at the same time.

Hammer pegs, however, will be needed in greater pro-portions since all the children from two upwards will like playing with them.

No child will play for long or very frequently with fitting toys; therefore, though it is a good thing to have a fair assortment of different kinds, many of each will not be needed. Picture trays and puzzles, we found, were the most popular of this type of play material.

A Nursery School Day

The kind of outdoor play place in a nursery school is as important as the toys and apparatus which are provided. It is absolutely essential for the children to have a garden, a real garden and not a dreary paved, asphalt or concrete playground. A garden essentially means living, growing things—a place full of life, plant and animal life. It is this vital quality of a garden which is so important, because it belongs naturally to outdoor and not indoor. All the materials of life, our food, our clothes, our houses and furnishings come from the good earth, and the children must experience the nature and qualities of the earth itself and the teeming life it yields. A concrete playground shuts out life as in a prison, a garden exhibits life in all its manifold properties.

But there are gardens and gardens. There are even beautiful gardens which we would not have, out of choice, as a play place for a crowd of small children! What do children need most in a garden? They need to have experience, as much experience as possible, and as varied experience as possible. Experience involves a great deal of experimenting and observation. We must therefore provide a number of different characteristics, or forms of matter, both living and inert and the space and tools for experiments.

A garden must have a number of properties, and none of them should be of the kind children will be told not to touch. There must be grass; not a small patch, for that would be worse than useless. If possible a grass bank is a great advantage; a few steps with a low wall on either side somewhere on that bank are very useful for physical balance and skill. The children need trees, and if some are good climbing trees what a stroke of luck for the nursery.

VIIa. Trains and Bricks. The best train has trucks for loading

VIIb. Pets. An excellent way of learning responsibility and kindness

VIIIa. Doll's Play. Improvised material and home-made dolls suffice for a successful tea-party

VIIIb. The Cot. A real hut of your own makes hard work worth while

A Nursery School Day

Trees not only give shade, and this is very necessary in the hot sun; they are an ever-fascinating store of equipment for the children, for they provide leaves, flowers and fruit, all of which will be put to a very good use. Shrubberies are always favourite play places, for they provide such excellent private 'hidy holes' for family games as well as yield the same rich material as trees. A few paths are necessary because it is such fun to practise 'keeping on the road' when you are riding a tricycle or pushing and pulling prams, carts or barrows.

It is essential, particularly with our damp climate, to have the part of the garden close to the school surfaced with some fairly hard material and well drained for wet weather use. There should also be beds for both flowers and vegetables, but not many. Last, but not by any means least, there must be a part of the garden where children can dig and make as much mess as they like with earth and water, making canals, pits, mountains and many other forms of construction their active minds and imagination will suggest to them.

That is the kind of garden nursery schoolchildren need to develop into healthy and active beings. In this garden they will also need other forms of play material. A sandpit and a climbing frame are absolutely essential. Next in importance come slide and paddling pool. If the latter is too expensive to build, old rubber or tin baths will do as well, provided there can be several in use at once in the summer-time.

The sandpit should be as big as it is possible to make it, for it will be in constant use by children of all ages. Any and all old kitchen utensils, pots, pans, wooden spoons, etc., will be just as popular as expensive 'sand toys' which are bought in shops. But there must be a large selection. Spades for digging should be strong and well made. It is better to have fewer good ones, of this article, than many cheap wooden ones which break easily.

There should also be a good selection of carts, trolleys, trucks, wheelbarrows, for use in and out of the sandpit. All carts, prams, barrows, trucks and trolleys will be used by the children for riding in. Therefore it is essential for all those provided to be sufficiently strong to carry a child. These toys should also be used for indoor play in wet weather. The use of passages is important for this type of play when it is impossible to be out of doors. Boxes are a very important item of garden equipment and are used more frequently than any other single thing. Their chief use is for imaginative and co-operative play and there is no limit to the number which can be used. Boxes and crates of all shapes and sizes are equally useful, but the bigger the better. Greengrocers are usually the best providers of wooden crates; it is always necessary to remove tin and wire bands, remove or hammer in nails which are sticking out, and to sandpaper the surface of the wood to remove possible splinters. The children will take great pleasure in painting some of the boxes if the grown-ups will provide the paint. Painting with real oil paint is naturally a thrilling occupation, but must be very carefully supervised by the adults, since oil paint is very difficult to remove. Swings, rings, ladders are also very good gymnastic apparatus to have, for these help tremendously in the physical development of the children and in giving them balance, confidence, and assurance, mentally as well as physically. Ladders should be small and short so that little children can carry them about easily. Planks for balance walking are also good, and if there are trees in the garden which the children can learn to climb, they should learn to climb as soon as possible. If they can get on to the walls round the school garden so much the better.

A Nursery School Day

There was a tree growing against the wall in the garden of my nursery school, and when the children discovered that they could climb into the tree and from there reach the wall, hardly a day passed without a string of them running along the top of the wall, asking to be 'jumped' down (for the wall was six feet high).

Tricycles and kiddicars are also necessary—tricycles, I find, are better than kiddicars, because they don't tend to overturn, and being better made their pedals always turn properly—which is very important.

Since it is much more convenient for the adults and even better fun for the children to use messy things in the garden than indoors, it is essential to have water available out of doors. It is an excellent plan to have a tap in the garden as well as a good-sized water tray. In the summer the children should spend all day out of doors. Sun-suits are, of course, ideal garments for playing with water in. Warm sunny days should be made good use of for this purpose. It is useful to have two sun-suits at school. Classroom materials can be taken out too, but they must be brought back and put away just as they are put away in the classroom itself.

In the summer, provided the weather is sufficiently warm, the children should spend the whole day in sun-suits. Naturally the transition from spring clothes to all-day sun-suits should take place gradually, but once used to sun-suits the children should wear them as much as possible; the sun-suits should be as scanty as possible, for it is very important in this country of relatively little sunshine to make the utmost use of every ray we can. Most children, if exposed to the sun very gradually, a little longer every day, and as early as possible in the summer, before the rays have become too hot, will tan a dark brown very quickly, and once brown run no risk of sunburn, however long they stay in a really hot July sun. There are, of course, children whose skin never tans. These obviously cannot run about in any sun with only a sun-suit; they should wear thin voile blouses or frocks over their sun-suits most of the time.

When playing in the garden with classroom materials which require a sedentary position the children should take them into the shade, particularly during the midday and early afternoon hours, for the glare of the sun is bad for their eyes, and heat beating down on a motionless body is much greater than when the children are running about. Usually the children seek out a shady spot of their own accord when they want to play with a 'quiet' toy.

ABOUT ANIMALS AND PLANTS

It is frequently said that young children should have pets and gardens, and as frequently that they shouldn't if they cannot, or will not, look after them themselves. Personally I think it is most important that children should have animals of some sort in their immediate environment, particularly dogs, of which so many children are frightened. Fear of animals comes very largely from lack of familiarity with other species which, while being alive and active like humans, are so different from them and therefore appear strange and terrifying to a small child.

Children who have a cat and/or dog in their family are not frightened of other cats and dogs, and usually show less fear of other animals. Having animals also widens the child's field of experience and interest, particularly in that of biological studies. The keeping of a pet or pets is also a source of great satisfaction to a child's 'will-to-power', for he feels as superior to the animals as he thinks adults are superior to him; he can mother them, protect them, and also bully and lord it over them, and naturally this is all very satisfying and perfectly natural and good so long as the animals are 'tactfully' protected by the adults from too much attention from the children. For the children it is really good, and they learn to care for and consider other beings who need their protection.

But this is no proof that children under six or seven should be held responsible for looking after an animal really properly. It would be asking far too much from children so young.

If the teachers in a nursery school, or the parents of a child, are prepared to give the time and attention required to keeping a pet or 'pets', it is well worth their while to do so; but they should hold themselves responsible and only ask the children to help and naturally encourage them to do so as much as possible. The children are usually interested, but that interest is naturally not sustained and comes and goes in spasms; it would be imposing an impossible burden on young children to expect them to give the necessary daily attention which is required by any living organism. Nevertheless, becoming familiar with the habits and ways of an animal and watching the adults tend it certainly helps very much to develop consideration and care in the children, so that they in their turn will become good 'tenders' themselves as they grow older.

What is true of animals is also true of flowers and plants.

Young children will not tend a garden properly or systematically; their interest will come and go. This is no reason for refusing them a 'garden' if they want one. It is often sufficient that an elder child should ask for a garden or be seen tending one for even two-year-olds to say, 'I want a garden', 'I want to plant flowers', and the whole group will want to do it.

And so they should; let them have an orgy of planting

seeds or plants; they will perhaps water them once or twice; but as a flower results only after many weeks after the planting of a seed a nursery-school child can hardly be expected to keep up his interest in an invisible process. Just as it is a good thing for the children to have animals about, so it is good for them to have plants and flowers about, that they may see them, watch them grow and change, learn to respect their rights (not to be trampled on or pulled up by the roots, for instance) and learn to tend them. But the real care of the flower-bed should be in the hands of the adults—so that there should be something real for the children to see and help care for. There should not, of course, be too much 'flower-bed' about the nursery school garden; most of it should be for the children's unrestricted use; just one flower-bed, or two, according to the size of the garden and the school, and one where the children can dig and plant exactly as they like.

It is important to grow vegetables as well as flowers in a nursery-school garden; the satisfaction of helping to produce, and watch grow, the actual food which you will eat at a real meal is qualitively different from producing flowers that you only look at. In making a choice of both flower and vegetable seed the adults should always remember that the quickest results are required. The best seed to provide is therefore that of plants which are hardy and grow rapidly; with flowers it is also important to remember that as soon as the buds appear the children will want to pick them. Therefore choose prolific flowering plants, such as marigolds, daisies, pansies, forget-me-nots, nasturtiums, sweet peas, etc. With vegetables the children will all want to 'have one each'; therefore choose small vegetables which you can grow *en masse*: such as lettuces, mustard and cress, carrots, and radishes. Peas and beans are also nice to grow, particularly as you can start them indoors in water and watch the roots grow. This is a great experience for small children and they will show interest in planting them out when the first leaves appear. For gardening the children should have tools just as strong and usable as those of the adults but of a size that is suited to them. It is always best for their tools to be kept in the tool-shed with the grown-up tools. The children will take greater pride in them, and therefore greater care, if this is done.

In a private garden, where most of it is in fact tended by adults and it is usually a case of 'No, you mustn't run there, you'll spoil the flowers', or 'Don't do that, Kate, there are bulbs coming up there', a child should have his own plot where he is free to do exactly as he likes; but even then the wise parent gives help and advice, for it is too difficult a task to be an efficient gardener at four or five years old. X once planted some daffodil bulbs when she was four; they came up, but, alas! they were flowerless. X was miserable, then she was angry, and went round and pulled up every plant. A really tactful parent helps to bridge the gap between planting and flowering in order to ensure success, for there is nothing more discouraging and heartbreaking to a small child than to see no result for hard work put in.

Domestic pets are by no means the only livestock of a garden; in fact they only make up a fraction of it, and not the most important section at that. A garden naturally abounds with insect life, and this is of great importance to small children; watching and collecting insects are two occupations which take up quite a good proportion of small children's time, energy and attention; they learn more from these activities than from nature lessons, even long after they have started their school life.

Chapter Six

THE SCHOOL CHILD

THE SLOW APPROACH TO SCHOOL WORK

THE law of continual progressive change is one of the most fundamental laws of nature. Men realize its validity in scientific work, but fail to apply it to themselves, particularly where children are concerned. We lightly talk of infancy, babyhood, childhood, adolescence as if a child overnight jumped from one condition to another.

Even if lessons are postponed until the beginning of the seventh year, the child must usually jump from fairly free play activity to a relatively long, organized school day. Even when the lesson period is not one of the three Rs but is devoted to handwork, dramatic work or story reading, it is still not of the children's choosing, nor is the content planned by them. It is essentially provided by the teacher. Children, who up till then had a garden to play in, or at least a park in the neighbourhood, have no more than a fifteen-minute break, herded together in a barren asphalt playground. Yet these children are still what they were the day before, what they had been for weeks and even months before and what they will be for many months to come. Change is slow, even if it is quicker in childhood than in adult years. Why then, cannot we recognize the slowness of growth, and make the first four or five years of school a slow and steady change from the nursery school? True, many infant schools, that is schools catering for children from five to seven years, do their best to make the break gentler, by trying to give the children some free activity periods in their school day. But the large classes and poverty of equipment make this very difficult in practice. Many schools do not even make this attempt.

The fortunate child that comes from a well-equipped nursery school or a home (one in a thousand) which has been able to supply all the equipment he needs, including playmates, has not at the age of six, let alone five, sufficient direct personal experience of the material world, living and dead (organic and inorganic) to be able to sit down, become interested in, and absorb information about different aspects of human knowledge chosen by adults.

Although children have enjoyed stories from early childhood and known that these are sometimes read out of books, they, the stories, still remain essentially in the realm of the spoken word.

Five-year-olds become really interested in the printed word; they notice big advertisements and ask what they 'say'. They want to read the names on Cornflake cartons; they learn by heart whole pages out of their favourite story books and 'read' them with great pride to admiring relatives. They are eager to learn their letters and to write their own and other people's names. Yet this interest is always spasmodic and easily displaced by suggestions for other kinds of play. Basically play, and active discovery and construction, are still the immediate interests of the five- and six-year-olds. Letters, words and numbers are beginning slowly to be incorporated into their view of the world and to take their place as meaningful symbols.

England is the only country in which the compulsory

school age is five years. In most countries it is six and in some it is seven. The large majority of children who begin learning to read at five, when they enter the infant school, cannot read fluently until they are eight, in spite of the fact that they spend the larger part of their school day at this task.

The majority of children who begin to read at seven learn in one year. This means that in practice, children who begin at five waste a great part of three years doing what they could have done in the last one of those years, while devoting the first two to other important activities.

Neither the five- nor the six-year-old has done more than begin to learn to handle tools and to learn the skills necessary for writing. Nor are they yet ready to develop as much interest in activities suggested by adults as their own. They are still living, to a large extent, in a world of their imagination. It cannot be otherwise until they have themselves reached, by dint of sheer growth as well as experience and practice of their skills, the near-adult stage of the pre-puberty years, say ten or eleven. So long as children are, in reality, rather helpless dependents, as indeed they are up to adolescence in our highly mechanized and complicated society, they must compensate for this inferiority by both make-believe and creation out of their own imagination.

Throughout the junior years the chief motive power behind children's eagerness to know and to become skilful is still the one they had in their earlier years, to become adult. Their conception of being adult is still hazy and consists more of being able to do all the things adults do in the home and to have the power to do as they like than of being literate and knowledgeable. These two last characteristics of being grown-up grow in importance as the children discover for themselves, in the course of their

The School Child

play and learning to use tools and make things, as well as in their attempts to understand the living world around them, that reading is the key to further knowledge about things they are interested in and is also the gateway into another world of exciting make-believe, that of stories, similar in some ways, but different in others, from their own world of fantasy play.

This discovery will only be made as early as six if a child has had the opportunity of experiencing good story reading for a long time and has had plenty of picture books himself, with large and attractive print. The desire to learn to read will not blossom out if his first eager questions about writing which has attracted his attention, are not satisfied.

Above all, children, whose first need is to be active, creative and constructive, are not likely to take to a sedentary life, concentrating on memorizing symbols unless their primary needs are also fulfilled. Besides, writing the letters of the alphabet requires very great muscular control, and children cannot achieve the necessary skill unless they have had a great deal of practice in drawing and painting.

PLAY NEEDS

Children who attend a primary school in which not much time is given to art or handwork and lessons have little activity about them, need to have this compensated for at home.

The need to play with creative handwork materials such as paints, clay, sand, paste and odd things such as dead matches, cartons, empty match boxes, pipe cleaners, cotton reels, is a priority, right up to adolescence.

Children also still require constructional toys, such as meccano, builder bricks, etc., and all kinds of models to make up in cardboard. The difference between constructional toys and materials for creative work is that the latter require imagination and originality and the former do not. Now far more energy, effort and concentration are required for imaginative work and children only have a limited amount of all three. It is therefore necessary for them to have a balance between the two so that they can do creative work when they are fresh and vigorous and have models and constructional equipment to fall back on when they need less difficult and exacting play.

Constructional toys are mostly fairly expensive to buy. Fortunately once a 'set' has been bought it will last more or less forever and can be added to all the time. But for parents who cannot afford any of these toys it is quite possible to make the one mentioned on page 56. For younger children the pieces can be quite simple, just short lengths of dowel rod and some cotton reels. For older children the constructions can be made more complicated by having bits of wood of all shapes and sizes drilled in various places for the dowel rod, as well as cotton reels, which can also be cut in different ways, and many lengths of rod.

Just because children up to ten and eleven are still dependent, and, relatively to adults, fairly ignorant, they still require to play imaginative games with building bricks, miniature cars, dolls and animals and dressing-up equipment. I am always reminded of this need by seeing the junior children in my school, sometimes tall for their age and looking very grown-up, coming in their play periods to play in the nursery department and always returning to the sandpit in the garden. There the play is naturally more mature than that of the pre-school children, and includes elaborate constructions such as dams, canals, watersheds, artificial streams, lakes, bridges, tunnels, etc. In their play the children not only satisfy their creative and imaginative needs, but also incidentally learn a great deal of science and geography which is none the worse for being unconscious.

Children between six and eleven naturally require far more in the way of creative materials than younger ones; but although paints, coloured pencils, paper and cardboard all cost a great deal nowadays, it is possible to provide much at little cost if the 'junk' from the household is systematically put aside for the children. Even scraps of wrapping paper, paper bags and newspapers are useful for papier-mâché work. Children from seven to eight are quite capable of making all kinds of things out of papier-mâché (paper made into a thick paste with cold water paste) from bowls to puppet heads. For glove puppets a solid clay head has to be made first, round which the cast of the papier-mâché is worked. It is then removed by being cut into two, when dry, either from centre back to centre front or from ear to ear.

From about six or seven onwards children need a few games such as 'ludo', 'lotto' and later on draughts and chess as well as ordinary playing cards and card games. Games, apart from draughts and chess, require much less thought and energy and are useful chiefly for the time when children are too tired after their day's activity or on rainy days when *all* the time cannot be spent creating and making. They are also very useful in learning the hard lesson of taking a beating in a competitive activity. Children enjoy competing against each other or in teams, and it is right and proper that they should, so long as this does not play an unduly important part for them or take priority over other play and activities. It should be the least important of their needs. The younger the child the less he can accept losing in such a game and that is one reason why that kind of game is not suitable for young children. But from the time a boy or girl clamours to play with the 'bigger' chil-

dren in a game of 'snap' or 'ludo' then he or she must
accept being a loser from time to time. In order to help a
'little' one to accept such a hard fate it is wise for adults
to take a part in the games and 'allow' the younger participant to win sufficiently often for him to feel he is a
success at games. He will then be more prepared to lose.
If children begin to quarrel over the results of a game it is
always wise to remove it and tell them that so long as they
are not big enough to accept the winners and losers it is
better for them not to play.

Play acting is also still very important to children right
up to eleven or twelve. It is one more aspect of their need
to play at being adult and powerful. It is a very therapeutic
activity for getting rid of a great deal of charged-up energy
and feeling about the adult world, which controls so many
of their actions and desires. It is easier to provide the older
children, say from nine onwards, with dressing-up materials, for they are old enough, from that age upwards, to
make quite a lot of their dresses themselves from bits of
materials or old clothes which they are given.

From six to ten or eleven children increase their skills at
a great rate, if they are given the opportunity of practising
them. Both boys and girls can become equally good at
carpentry. They can successfully use a screwdriver, a hand
drill and a chisel as well as with a coping saw and fret saw
by the time they are ten. They can make quite useful things
for themselves as well as toys and models. Both can equally
succeed with sewing, weaving and knitting, and both are
equally pleased with their achievements, provided the
adults have the right attitude towards that kind of work.

In all their creative activities, as well as their play acting,
children need the interest and encouragement of adults. If
the grown-ups consider the children's creations as meaningless and useless, their painting and clay models as 'silly'

because the things they mean to represent are badly drawn or modelled, then the children will become discouraged and give up making the effort which these creative activities require. If the grown-ups simply ignore them the children have less incentive to work, put less effort into the things they do, give up more quickly and are generally much less ambitious in their projects. If the adults are prepared to take an interest in the things the children make or do, and offer to help and advise when they are asked, the children will be far happier and will achieve more, with less fuss and bother, less quarrelling, and less upset. Throughout the junior years children need as much outdoor playtime as younger children for they are still growing rapidly, even though less rapidly than before. They need exercise for all their limbs which cannot be provided indoors unless it is in a gymnasium. Even the fortunate children who can go to a gym do not get the right equipment for their exercise. It is always better for a young child to be climbing a tree or negotiating a fence, because, apart from the activity being carried out in the open air, it is being done in a context which carries excitement, pleasure and interest, which are not present in a gymnasium atmosphere, however good it may be. A child requires this exercise daily; this is pursued not for its own sake, but in the course of some game. He also needs it, as he did in his pre-school days, as much for confidence in himself as for exercise for his limbs, and the gaining of skill and balance.

OUTDOOR GAMES AND SKILLS

All children between six and ten should have the opportunity of learning to ride a bicycle and to swim. It is not simply that these are useful skills to have at one's command, nor even that exercising them is good for health. The important thing is confidence in himself, which a child achieves through learning them. Children gain poise, assurance, and security as well as the thrill of success in mastering skills which are really difficult and dangerous!

The child also needs the opportunity to discover more of the mysteries of nature, and the physical laws which govern the world. With the most rich and helpful environment and adults always ready to explain and show why and how things work, a child has barely time before he enters secondary school to learn sufficiently at first hand of the nature of our earth, and its living matter, to have a basis on which to build up and understand the content which will be given him to learn in his history, geography and science lessons at school. It is for this reason, as well as their need for the interest and encouragement of the adults that young children should be taken out as often as possible on holidays, for excursions to see or hear things of interest, such as trips to the docks, to the countryside, to see trains, exhibitions, museums, to spend a day on the river, go to the seaside or hills or mountains. For children who live all the year round in a city, a weekly Sunday picnic in the summertime just outside the town is a real thrill. Even London, which stretches its giant tentacles miles out along the land, can be left behind. I know of at least four or five little rivers (perhaps streams would be a better name) set in pleasant fields which can be reached in a half-hour's train or bus ride from London. Country children, on the contrary, need to be taken in to see the sights of a town and visit museums and exhibitions. Both country and town children need the grown-ups to share their interests and answer the eager questions they ask about all they see, as well as help them to find the answers to those questions the adults cannot answer.

The school child wants to get as messy and dirty as the

The School Child

pre-school one, though he will do it in slightly different ways. Weather does not affect him as much as it does a little boy or girl. The younger child gets cold, and hence less active, much quicker and more easily than an older one. So in the winter months, particularly if they are wet, the little children will be less eager to run out to play and get dirty in the garden or countryside. The older, seasoned school boy or girl will, on the contrary, often welcome rain because it is such fun to get wet and splash about in puddles. It is quite remarkable how late in life the desire to stamp about in puddles continues! Neither rain nor cold prevent healthy, lively children from wanting to climb, play games, explore, as well as dig and build in sand and earth and construct hide-outs and shelters for themselves out of old boxes, planks, sacks and old blankets which they can beg and borrow from the grown-ups.

BOOKS FOR THE SCHOOL CHILD

When reading is begun seriously it is a great encouragement for a child to be given attractive picture books with not too much print on each page; small books with a few pages so that the print can be memorized very quickly and the child can feel a pride in having read a whole book from beginning to end. Folk tales are excellent stories to learn because there is a great deal of repetition in them; stories such as the *Gingerbread Boy*, *The House that Jack Built*, *Titty and Tatty*, *Billy Goat Gruff* and so on. This is, of course, not systematic reading, but it is a great spur to a child to put effort into his lessons because he knows what letters make, what words strung together make, and the fun and glory of being able to read some meaningful sentences. Another way of stimulating a desire to learn more is to play games with the phonic alphabet, letters with matching pictures. There are no games of this kind on the market, but it is quite easy to make picture lottos with cardboard and pictures cut out of magazines or even alphabet books and a set of cut-out letters in wood or plastic. A further step in this line is a game with three-and four-letter words (phonic ones, naturally) and pictures of the words they spell: another game can be made up with separate letters, and a group of five or six pictures of objects with easy phonic names, such as cat, well, pig, dog and so on. 'I spy with my little eye' is a game which all children have probably enjoyed for generations and is the best way of all to learn the sounds of the letters. For children who have learnt most of their letter sounds, can build monsyllabic phonically regular words and have learnt the basic 'looksay' words for simple reading, the Gay Colour books by E. R. Boyce make excellent first story books."

Reading to children who are learning their letters is always a stimulus to work. Boys and girls are now beginning to differentiate quite clearly between reality and make-believe and want their stories to belong to one or the other. They enjoy both kinds, but do not like confusion. When they listen to stories about history or geography or nature study they always ask eagerly: 'Is it true?' 'Did it really happen?' 'Could it happen like that?' When they listen to fairy stories, and the early junior years are those for fairy tales, although they live themselves into the story as it is being told, when something dangerous or frightening occurs they quickly reassure themselves by saying very firmly and very loudly: 'Of course, that isn't true at all; there aren't any witches really, are there?' The tradional fairy-tales, particularly Grimm's tales, are not suitable, even for junior children, for the frightening elements are sometimes very strong. But many of them are folk tales which are somewhere halfway between magic and reality and make

The School Child

excellent literature for the youngest school children, just as myths and legends are suitable for the older, ten- and eleven-year-olds. All countries have a literature which is rich in folklore, and it is possible to buy collections of such tales from many countries. The Brer Rabbit stories are a classic example of stories from the negro people of the Southern States of North America. The Epaminondas stories also give great delight to six- and seven-year-olds. Both before children have learnt to read, and afterwards, the books which are read to them by adults should always be carefully chosen for their quality of language as well as their suitability for that age. They should be simply but well written, with a vocabulary well within the grasp of the children who are to hear them. Books in which the author writes down to children are no good at all. Morality should be implicit, never explicit. Children do not want to be preached at. Books that are popular with six- and seven-year-olds, apart from fairy tales and folk tales, are those by Beatrix Potter and Alison Uttley. Children as young as this enjoy the everyday doings of other children because they so easily identify themselves with the characters in the story.

Another series which appeals to young children for much the same reason, although the heroine is a bear, are the Mary Plain books by G. Rae. There are many excellent story books for school children ranging from 5 to 12 years of age, written by authors such as Ardizzone, Bemelmans, Duvoisin, de Brunhoff, Flack, Francoise, Trease, Nesbitt, Ransome, and others for the older primary school child.

Many people think that once a boy or girl can read fairly fluently he or she need not be read to any more, and parents sigh with relief because they think they will be spared the daily task of story reading. This is a great mistake. Children continue to need being read to right up to secondary school age. Even after fluency has been achieved, reading with understanding requires effort and concentration. Books using a vocabulary which is considerably smaller than that which the child himself uses need this effort to be understood completely. Story reading from an adult continues to stimulate interest and the ambition to read more difficult books for the sake of their content. They also should give children practical experience of good elocution. So much of children's reading must, of necessity, be done silently, that there is always the danger of their reading being, at best, monotonous, and at the worst downright incorrect and slipshod. There is a quality in reading aloud which is quite absent in silent reading, and which, if the book being read is a good one, brings out the dramatic and exciting properties of the story, so that children see it in a new and more thrilling light.

Adults should quite deliberately choose, for reading aloud to children over seven years of age, books which, in both content and language, are just beyond the child's own reading capacity. Because the child does not have to make the effort to read, he is free to put all his concentration into following the actual story and understanding the use of words and phrases. This effort is a great help in encouraging children to become interested in more difficult and advanced books and to want to read more of them.

The most important quality of stories for children of pre-puberty years is action. Children are not interested in the creation of 'atmosphere'. through subtle descriptive passages, nor in strong silent characters who never say a word, nor in people who talk all the time and do nothing. There must be constant action and conversation which explains or leads to this action. It must also be the kind of action which is understood by children and which they themselves either enjoy doing or would like to do. Traditional fairy-tales as well as myths and legends have that quality about them, even though they are make-believe. The fantasy is of doing and being that which the young children dream of and long for. Trease is a writer of historical fiction for children who shows in his books the qualities of direct action and choice of characters which appeal immediately to children. But he uses a difficult vocabulary and his language is that of older children, say twelve or thirteen years. Yet the contents of his books are very suitable for nine- and ten-year-olds. Ransome is a seafaring man who has a great understanding of children and the boating adventures of his famous family have all the qualities which appeal to boys and girls who love adventure and the countryside.

The children's classics, which accumulate as the generations go by, each leaving its small quota behind, have acquired honour through those very qualities of appealing to childhood, and they remain popular however old they are. It is important, however, to give children *Alice in Wonderland*, Kipling's *Jungle Books*, *Black Beauty*, *Tom Sawyer* or any other classic at the right moment and not too early. It has been my experience that parents, relatives and friends, tend to give children most of these books several years before they are ready for them. The effect of this is disastrous because not only is the child disappointed at the time he receives the gift, but the book never regains its rightful place in the child's eyes; it is usually spoilt for good. This is a pity, for our children's classics constitute the first steps to the reading of good serious literature in later days and surely this is what we all want to encourage.

Chapter Seven

THE DISCIPLINE OF LATER CHILDHOOD

THE DEMANDS OF SCHOOL, CUSTOM AND TRADITION

FOR the baby, until he is about two years old, social discipline, as distinct from natural discipline of physical laws, consists almost entirely of a series of items chosen, quite arbitrarily as far as he is concerned, by the grown-ups which are either tabu or must be performed. The baby does not know why or wherefore, but simply 'that is what Mummy or Daddy or who you will, wants', and the baby either does it willingly because he has no strong feelings either way or enjoys it or wants to please the adult, or he is made to do it (or stop doing it, as the case may be) by force. For example, little babies hate having their faces washed, but their faces must be washed all the same. Mother may use one of two techniques; either she does it as quickly as possible and comforts the baby afterwards or she prolongs the agony by trying, dur-the operation, to distract the baby's attention and get him to put up with it without tears. A two-year-old has grown out of that unpleasant and humiliating position of dependence and takes a great pleasure in washing his own face and hands. Later on the situation is once more reversed.

After three or four years of age washing has returned to the infancy stage, it is an unpleasant, and, to the child quite senseless, occupation. But there is this difference, that the child is now both able to fulfil the task himself and to understand the reason for it, though he himself does not accept the reason!

Between two and five or six years a very significant change has taken place in the child. His developing intelligence, his growing experience, and above all his use and understanding of speech, have brought him to the stage of reasoning, judging and understanding a great deal of causality. All this, of course, does not happen overnight, but is a long and often painful process, spread over years, as the chapter on nursery discipline shows.

By the time a child is six and has been helped both by adults and other children to control his behaviour when it threatens to become anti-social or destructive, to conform to a home routine and accept its sanctions because both are not too severe and respect his rights and needs, then he should be ready to welcome and accept the far more exacting demands of the school years.

Just as we often underestimate the little child's difficulty in grasping causal significance and understanding the adult's viewpoint, so do we underestimate the demands that are made of the school child. From five or six onwards the pressure from the adult world on the child to hasten his rate of mental and emotional growth is very great. Pressure comes from home and from school. The pressure from the school is largely due to the fact that at the secondary stage education in England is still partly selective and that there are nothing like sufficient schools offering what is popularly accepted as good education, whether State or independent. Although we now have unselective Comprehensive Secondary Schools in the greater part of

The Discipline of Later Childhood

England, most of the grammar schools still in fact operate on a selective examination level, and many countries have not yet gone comprehensive. So the primary school still has its function, in practice, to try to secure, for some of its pupils, places in the 'academic' schools. So the primary school has as its function, in practice, if not in theory, to try to secure for its pupils the two places out of ten in the 'academic' secondary schools. This attempt to raise the academic standards of children to the point at which each one hopes to beat those of his neighbour in the race, imposes almost intolerable conditions for the great majority of children. These conditions are reflected in the children's attitudes to discipline as well as to lessons. The pressure from home, although partly due to the same anxiety on the parent's part that their boy or girl shall get into a good secondary school, shows itself in practical ways in the sphere of behaviour rather than of accomplishments. Since it is not the parents' task to teach the child its lessons, fathers and mothers only express opinions about these, but where the child's behaviour in everyday life is concerned the parents are in direct control.

Just because we are social beings we are sensitive to the opinions of our neighbours. We all want to be approved of and our children are a part of ourselves. So all of us, some more than others, some consciously, some unconsciously, want our children to behave in such a way that they shall be approved of by the neighbours and by the relations. New ideas, new social ways of living and thinking slowly emerge from the existing pattern of social life. At first only a few accept and believe in the new ideas; the majority always continue holding on to traditional ways of life, because these are symbols of security and reliability.

Changes in social customs, beliefs and ideas come about as a result of man's ever-growing understanding and control over nature which alters his way of living. The change in the attitude of adults to children has come about partly through the decrease in sizes of families during the past fifty years. Smaller families have meant that more attention, care and consideration could be given to the existing children. Better education has led a large number of parents to understand and to voice their demand for information about their children. This and the need for dealing effectively with persons who break down in mental health has led to a great deal of very active work in the field of child psychology during the past thirty or forty years.

The result of all this work has been the recognition that children have very specific needs of their own which must be studied, understood and satisfied if the children are to grow up healthy, capable and socially well intergrated in society. But the recognition of these needs and how they are to be met has not yet become part and parcel of the general social pattern of life. So that parents who do recognize their validity are faced with disapproval from a large section of society if and when they put into practice these ideas on child upbringing. I well remember how very uncomfortable I felt, I may even say ashamed, when my child's behaviour in public, although I knew it was perfectly right, was frowned upon by the very respectable persons in the audience. How often have I had grave doubts about the wisdom of a certain course of action with children, because so many people have shaken their heads and prophesied that no good could come of it? The pressure of public opinion is very strong and public opinion is only beginning to change, although it has moved quite a way from the days when it was thought children should be seen and not heard.

The Discipline of Later Childhood

There are two overwhelmingly important reasons why children are willing to accept discipline, and these reasons have existed from the time they were born. The first is the wish to become adult, and that is synonymous with 'all powerful', the second is to be socially acceptable. Throughout childhood the drive to satisfy the primary egotistical needs must sometime come into conflict with the needs of others or society as a whole. When a child is faced with such a conflict the issue will be largely determined by the strength of the antagonistic pulls. Other things being equal, the pull of personal needs in the earliest years is stronger than the will to grow up (conscious will that is), but the need to be loved and the corresponding anxiety lest he should be rejected are both far stronger in younger than older children. It is therefore far easier to obtain 'good' behaviour from a small child by using the threat of 'rejection' towards behaviour which the grown-ups disapprove of. This is, of course, extremely dangerous because, basically, it rests on fear, and useless because when the child has outgrown his fear of 'rejection', behaviour which has so far been controlled by this fear will no longer be thus controlled. Even worse, the child who has been sufficiently frightened in this way may cease to have any initiative of his own, and only be able to do what his mother tells him. Yet we still often hear mothers saying, 'Mummy won't love you any more if you go on doing that.'

As a child grows older the dependence on adults decreases as he becomes more able to manage and do things for himself and his fear of rejection diminishes in proportion. But his need to be socially acceptable to other children increases as his need for them as playmates and companions appears with speech and growing experience. As his understanding of his inferior position grows with know-ledge and experience so does his desire to gain the skills and knowledge of adults. His need for companionship and playmates compels him to curb his own wishes and drives in favour of other children, to become generous, considerate and helpful so that others will desire and welcome his company. His wish to be adult drives him to accept the self-discipline necessary to learn facts and skills.

But what happens when a child has reached the age of five or six, so disillusioned about life that he has no wish to grow up at all? When contact with other children has been so painful that he shuns them and retreats into a shell of his own, putting up a façade of indifference? Here again the responsibility must be with the adults. Of course, some children are by nature more sociable than others, some are far more ambitious than others, but all have some ambition and all are sociable to some extent. Children who have lost one or both of these characteristics are ill, mentally sick, because of the way in which the world has met their early tentative contacts. If, during the junior years, when the pressure to learn and behave in a civilized manner is becoming very strong, the adults cannot appeal to a desire to become grown-up or the desire for friendship with other children they have no means at their disposal to awaken (or evoke) a desire for the self-discipline which is so necessary to achieve these ends. The child's whole attitude to life (including human society) must be re-examined and the adult world must help him to regain his confidence in himself and society. Only then can any discipline become effective for that child.

Even so, we must realize how difficult it is for the young child of school age to accept voluntarily the constant

The Discipline of Later Childhood

control of himself which learning at school and behaving with almost grown-up standards at home demands of him.

All children of over six years are quite capable of understanding the reasons for simple rules of social conduct, such as not shouting others down, being reasonably polite, not grabbing or snatching things for yourself or pushing people out of the way. But understanding a reason is not the same as putting the rule into effect. Children usually want to behave in a social way because they want approval, but they so often forget. It is not usually necessary to do more than remind them constantly of the simple rules when they forget them. Sometimes it may be necessary to impose a social consequence when a rule is infringed too frequently, such as being deliberately helped last or given the smallest cake when grabbing the best for himself. Bad table manners are best met with the request that he or she should eat somewhere away from the others so that those need not suffer his or her presence. Above all, we should not expect better behaviour from our school-age children than we show ourselves. These children are well able, after the age of six, to judge us and our actions. If we ask them to do a job of work in the home, but rarely do one ourselves, if we ask them to get up at 7.30 but stay in bed ourselves, tell them not to shout but shout at them ourselves, how can we expect them to do these things? If we set our children an example of behaviour, we have gone a long way to get it back from them and we have, as well, a strong argument to use in our attempt to elicite it from them. If we have shown understanding of, and respect for, their rights in the family, given them their play space and material for work, listened to what they have to say to us, made allowances for bad moods, jealousies, disappointments and failures, without over-indulgence, we will find in practice that children at this age will accept sanctions and social consequences for their actions, whether these are due to thoughtlessness or deliberate desire to be 'bad'. We can only learn by experience; this is just as true in the sphere of social behaviour as in that of gaining knowledge. Children must learn this way and we help them by making clear to them the steps to mature controlled behaviour and the consequences of infringing these steps. If we fail to make these clear to them then we are failing the children as much as when we make the rules intolerably hard and meaningless.

When a child's behaviour has been sufficiently anti-social to require restraint or suffering the 'punishment' of the consequences of his action, it is absolutely essential that the adults should make it quite clear that it is not the child himself who is disapproved of, but his present behaviour. This is particularly important when a child has to be removed from others. Furthermore young children find it hard, almost impossible, to 'come back' into the community after they have been rejected for some aspect of behaviour. It is usually necessary for the grown-ups to make the first gesture. This should be made, in due course, after the child has recovered from his bad feeling, as if nothing had happened. To refer to the past conduct by saying something like 'You won't be a bad boy any more, will you?' can only have the devastating effect of reminding the child that his behaviour had been disapproved of and may start a bad scene all over again.

STEALING AND LYING

Stealing and lying are relative to the stage of development of a child. A baby has no idea of either since he has no idea of a difference between yours and mine nor between truth and untruth. His capacity to differentiate between his own possessions and those of others appears before his ability to distinguish between truth and fiction. Having at last grasped the distinction, he has still to learn to respect it. The temptation to seize what he wants is naturally very strong in a child and it takes several years for him to learn to control his desires. Here, again, he needs help from others in the shape of praise and encouragement when he resists a temptation, and sympathetic treatment when he has taken something from another and is made to give it back. Children who have a reasonable number of possessions of their own and have plenty of love and affectionate interest from their parents soon learn to resist the temptation to take what belongs to another or the community as a whole. Children who are deprived, more of affection and attention than of property, are those who cannot control their need to steal, and who steal not only things they want, but useless things which satisfy only the need to steal.

It is the same with lying. A child's recognition of the difference between the truth and a lie grows very slowly indeed. His fantasy is part of his life and as real to him at the time he invents it as anything which is happening in the world around him. He only outgrows this fantasy world as he gradually learns the laws of reality and can judge the creations of his fantasy by the light of the reality he has come to know. This takes a long time and the child who finds reality too frightening or painful and runs away from it takes longer to disentangle his imaginings from what really is. Lying to make yourself appear better, bigger, grander and so on, is a tendency common to all children, which disappears as the child grows older and as he finds adults prefer him as he is rather than as he tries to make himself out to be.

Lying to avoid detection is in a different category. Here again little children who have done something or taken something which they know they should not have done, will almost instinctively deny their action because confession would mean 'trouble' and it is instinctive in human nature to avoid pain. All small children do this; it is natural. Just because it is natural to try to avoid unpleasant consequences adults must show patience and understanding in helping children to realize the social need for truth in these matters. There are two ways of doing this; one is by not punishing the offence at all, or making the punishment very light, when the child has confessed to committing it, the other is by explaining to the child that by lying or keeping silent about an action he destroys other people's confidence in him. It may be necessary to let him experience this lack of confidence and mistrust by not accepting his word on a future occasion.

Stealing and lying are disastrously anti-social in their consequences, and it is this aspect of them which makes them so bad. They express, at its worst, the failure of a member of a community to curb his personal and egotistical needs when they threaten to infringe the rights of others. Now very small children are unaware of separate identities or of anyone's rights; it takes several years of learning and experience to gain this knowledge and once more it is the adult's responsibility to see to it that this experience is gained intelligently and reasonably. By the age of ten or eleven children should know and understand quite clearly the social reason for refraining from theft and lies, and should have learnt to control the temptation to give way to both.

One day four ten-year-old boys broke a cloakroom window by playing indoors with a football. They had frequently been told not to play with balls indoors because of the danger of breaking things. The accident occurred a few minutes before the end of school at 4.0 p.m. and

The Discipline of Later Childhood

no adult had witnessed it. The four boys went off home, saying good-bye to their teacher at the school gate. Two of them decided, when they were halfway down the road, to turn back and confess the accident. This they did, being, naturally, careful to say that neither of them had been responsible for the actual breakage! The next day the children's action was discussed with the whole class and all the children were asked their opinion of the behaviour of the four separate boys. Without any prompting from the teachers, the children said: 'The ones who didn't confess should pay a bigger part of the cost of repairing the window.' Then one boy suddenly said: 'You can't trust people who break things and then lie about them. My mother didn't believe me the other day when I really hadn't done what she said I had, because I had lied about spending some money.' The adults told the four responsible for the broken window that its repair would cost quite a lot of money. Then several other children in the class said that they had played with balls indoors on other occasions, if not on that one and that they were therefore also responsible, and in the end the majority of the children undertook to pay for the new window. If children are made, by practical experience, to understand the social consequences of acts of stealing and lying, that is the very best way of helping them to stop committing such actions.

Chapter Eight

THE SCHOOL CHILD'S SOCIAL LIFE

THE IMPORTANCE OF SOCIAL REALTIONSHIPS
BETWEEN CHILDREN

THE sternest test of discipline in childhood is always the child's capacity to behave sociably with his peers. His capacity to behave reasonably with adults and to accept the adult discipline of home and school are a lesser test. It is easier for a young child to make a compromise with the adult world, or to make no compromise at all, but allow himself to be ruled, and reserve for himself the possibility of breaking out against the adults if and when he feels like it. The world of adults is in a far stronger position than the child, so that the struggle of adaption is unequal and children, knowing this, are often able and willing to give an appearance of conformity to adult demands, without in fact accepting these demands in their true personalities. We all know that most children up to adolescence have quite different standards of behaviour, language and actions when they are alone together, to those they reveal in the presence of grown-up people. There are many children who, on the surface, appear to be well behaved and 'good', who are quite unable to play with other children because the demands which group play makes on every member of the community are both severe and inescapable. A child who refuses to share equipment or give up his ideas and plans in favour of those of another, who accepts no leadership but his own and who cannot lose cheerfully will always find himself finally rejected by the group, an outcast from society.

Learning to play with others, and, to a lesser extent, to work with others, is a very long and often painful process, as Chapter Two shows. It is something over which all children need help, right into the teens. This need runs counter to the tacitly accepted convention that school children loyally stand by one another in opposition to adults who also, in their turn, stand loyally by each other, in opposition to the children, enemies facing one another. It also contradicts the other accepted convention, which follows naturally from the first, that tale-telling is in itself a wicked and shameful thing to do. Tale-bearing is only shameful when it is used as a deliberate means of getting another child, or children, into trouble with the adults, that is to say, when it is used with cruel intent. It is then but one aspect, among others, of cruelty and bullying. When the tale bearing is used by a child, or children, as an attempt to secure justice and help in a situation which has got beyond their control, i.e. when a child is bullying or hurting another and the other children themselves cannot restrain him, then it is the right and proper thing to do. The nature of the relationship between children and adults is reflected in the attitude of the grown-ups towards tale bearing. Once children have outgrown the nursery years and the more obvious physical dependence on adults, we tend to expect them to be far more mature and independent than they really are. All change in nature is slow and gradual and this is no exception to the rule.

The School Child's Social Life

Our adult society, moreover, is certainly not such a shining example of all the Christian virtues that we can rely on the behaviour of the grown-ups whom the children know, see, hear or read about in the daily press, radio and television, to show them the way to behave towards each other!

If they are to be helped to become socially well adjusted, children must feel that the adult world is always on their side, even if this is expressed by restraining and even punishing their behaviour if it is anti-social. Children are realists, and from three years onwards their understanding of anti-social behaviour grows both in depth and breadth, particularly when the adults take pains to make the nature and consequences of such behaviour clear to the children themselves.

Because the relationship of adults to children is an unequal one, the grown-up being in authority and in control, activities with adults, including games played with adults, do not call for these qualities of voluntary self-control required in co-operative occupations with other children. We are therefore faced with the fact that children must be able to play freely together without adults, but on the other hand must feel always able to appeal to the adults when their behaviour leads them into social situations which cause pain, tears and fears. In practice this is not such a difficult thing to achieve, at least not in the home, since children are normally free to arrange and plan their out-of-school hours. It is far more difficult to achieve in school, because school hours are almost always organized by the adults. And yet, by its very nature, school should be in the best position to help, since teachers are always there

The School Child's Social Life

and since educating the children is their responsibility, they should always be able to deal with any situation which might arise. Out of school time the children are frequently away from the adults, who are therefore not available in an emergency, or find it difficult if not impossible to sort out the rights and wrongs of the affair, or are inevitably biased because they are parents or friends of some of the participants.

MORE LASTING FRIENDSHIPS

The years from six or seven till eleven are crucial ones with regard to becoming socialized; as children grow out of babyhood and dependence on adults they turn for companionship to their peers. If this contact is not successful and a child feels himself to be an outcast from his group, in the years of 'gang' companionship, he will almost certainly find the problems and difficulties of adolescence more difficult to overcome.

In the nursery years children's friendships are fleeting and unstable. A best friend at the beginning of a school day may be a bitter enemy at the end of a few minutes, and a best friend again by dinner-time. Social play is usually between two or three, rarely more than four children. It is as if they cannot at that age deal with the demands and needs of more than two or three of themselves at a time. By the time children are six or seven years old both their demands and their capacity for satisfying these demands have broadened to make large group games possible. Already individual children begin to show capacity for leadership, interest in organizing others, initiative and imagination in planning games and activities. This does not necessarily mean that these children are little dictators, though they may sometimes be 'bossy', for real leadership involves the ability to recognize different qualities in

152

individual persons and to bring these out by assigning to each a role in which he or she will be successful. The crucial test of whether a child is a real leader, or is merely ordering others about, lies in the attitude of the other children. If these accept the leadership of the one who is trying to lead, then it is the right kind of leadership. If the other children allow themselves to be browbeaten or intimidated into following one child, then it is not real leadership, but bullying.

No child who is unhappy and maladjusted can become a really successful leader. Just as the neglected child finds himself driven into all kinds of bad behaviour to gain notice and even notoriety, so he finds himself applying all his abilities to gaining power over other children to get them to help him in his bad deeds.

The need for social recognition from your peers is quite different in childhood from social recognition from the adults. The latter springs primarily from the dependence on the grown-ups; if the adults disapprove of you they might let anything happen to you—might even let you die! You must keep on the right side of them; besides you cannot help but have quite special feelings for adults, such as mother and father and other relatives who care for you day by day. The need for the good will of fellow dependents springs from quite another source, the basic need of humans for companionship in work and play. The price we have to pay for this, the greatest quality of man, which sets him unmistakably above all other animal life, is a degree of self-control which children do not have to achieve in their relationship with adults.

The School Child's Social Life

HELPING CHILDREN TO HAVE THE RIGHT
SOCIAL APPROACH

In relationships between equals give and take must be evenly matched. Small children, when they first consciously seek the friendship of other children of their own age, are naïve and assume that this can be bought with gifts (they themselves love their parents even more when these give them presents). Five- and six-year-olds are frequently heard to say: 'If I give you my dinky car will you be my friend?' 'Here is my new penny, will you play with me?' It is only through experience of playing together that children learn that real friendship is not bought with gifts, but by a capacity for forgetting self interests and entering into the interests of another. How difficult this is, any honest adult will admit, even after childhood is left behind. Children who, at the age of two and three have had no help from friendly adults in their early contacts with other children, or who have been teased or bullied by older children who have not been checked, or who have been allowed to behave anti-socially themselves, including anti-social behaviour towards other children, without restraint from the adults, find it extremely hard to learn to change their behaviour later on, or to go out to meet others with confidence and friendliness.

Cruelty and unkindness towards other children also result from lack of attention and affection from adults, or from adults' wrong handling of children's needs, particularly their play needs. A child that has been unnecessarily frustrated and checked in what can be regarded as his quite legitimate actions, such as playing with messy things, climbing trees and so on, which may involve dirty and torn clothes, usually has his unconscious revenge by imposing similar frustrations and checks on other, more helpless, children.

The exact opposite treatment from adults, that of over indulging a child, may have the same effect on that child's treatment of other children. Over indulgence means that parents have failed to help the child, from the earliest stage, to control his behaviour towards other humans in such a way as to be socially acceptable and welcome. The adults have not only failed to check behaviour which hurt others, they have also failed to show the children how to be kind to others. These two tasks are equally important. Children need the active help from the grown-up world just as much in their social relations with other children as in their learning about the material world of things. To deny this positive help and guidance from adults is to deny one aspect at least of evolution. To allow children to play absolutely freely without the slightest interference from adults means in practice, the law of the jungle, in which the strongest, both physically and mentally, beat up the less strong. Society as a whole has not yet learnt the way to real social living, how should we then suppose that children can learn even the simplest rules of good comradely living without the help of adults?

Nor is it sufficient to accept the fact that this help is required. The nature of the help is of great importance, both in the negative and positive spheres. In the negative by making the restraint of anti-social behaviour take the form of a social consequence rather than an arbitrary punishment inflicted by the adult. The latter does not give the child any help in understanding what was wrong with the behaviour for which he has been punished. The effect on the punished child is to make him hate the child he has already hurt because he considers him to be the cause of the punishment and the nett result is to make the child

The School Child's Social Life

more anti-social than he was before. If, on the other hand, the punishment takes the form of repair to, or replacement of anything damaged or lost, when this is the nature of the anti-social act committed, or removal from the other child or children when physical pain has been inflicted, with verbal explanations to reinforce the obvious logic of the adult's behaviour, then it is far more difficult for the child to deceive himself into blaming the child he has hurt. In fact it helps the child to face the reality of his behaviour, and this, in its turn, helps him to control himself in order to be 'liked'.

On the positive side, the adult, having more knowledge and experience than the young child, can often show or tell him the kind of behaviour on his part which will gain him the friendship and goodwill of others, how to co-operate in games and play, what activities to suggest, what roles to assign to another and so on. The younger the child, the easier it is for grown-ups to stop a quarrel or fight and help the children to either start a new game, or continue the old on the basis of a settlement suggested by the adult. Since play is the most important part of life for the pre-adolescent it is natural that play should be the most important aspect of his social life and the sphere in which he is most anxious to please and secure for himself friend-ship and co-operation. It is therefore doubly important for children to have free, yet supervised, playtime and equip-ment, not only during the nursery years, but well into the pre-puberty school years.

PERSONAL AND GROUP RESPONSIBILITIES

The play which has begun between three and six years in small groups of two, three or four, the bond of friendship and co-operation lasting in most cases only for the duration of that game, grows into more serious and permanent associations as the children grow older, more independent of adults, more self-confident and assured, but above all, more self-controlled and conscious of how to behave socially with one another. The experience of past years has built up a secure and solid consciousness of the advantages, the benefits and the help which they give one another in co-operative activity. It is, I believe, from this social experience in play that children carry over friendly and helpful co-operation into work situations. If there has been a failure on the child's part to achieve a capacity for social play, he will fail to achieve it in work, whether it is school work or the communal tasks for the community in which he lives. He will also fail to identify himself with his community, and consequently refuse to accept either the responsibilities of membership or the tasks imposed by membership. As children grow older the responsibilities placed upon them by the adult world naturally grow in proportion. There are, broadly speaking, two distinct groups of responsibilities; one consists of personal responsibilities, that is those connected with one's own personal relationships with other individuals; the other of group social responsibilities connected with the everyday life and welfare of the community (or communities) in which the children live.

Of these two groups the first and easiest to be achieved is the personal one. From the earliest age the small child has to begin the voluntary control of his behaviour in order to achieve friendship with other children and the approval of adults. From these small beginnings blossoms out the capacity to carry quite heavy personal responsibilities for others. Yet even to achieve responsibilities in personal relationships a child has, from the beginning, to feel that he is welcomed and loved for his own sake, because of his own personal qualities and character.

The School Child's Social Life

The acceptance of social and group responsibilities come as a result of the growing consciousness of the existence of the community and a child's own participation in that community. Naturally the family is the first group of several persons united by a common bond of which a child becomes aware, because he himself is one of the members. The measure of his capacity to become a responsible member of his family group is the direct measure of the degree of respect for his abilities and regard for his needs which he has received. If all his efforts to control his behaviour in a sociable manner are met with praise and his lapses with kindly help; if he is given an ever-increasing measure of responsibility as mental and physical powers grow, the strength of his group membership feeling will grow stronger and deeper.

The two chief reasons for the strength of the child's feeling for the family bond are: (1) the importance of each member to the others and the affection and close interdependence of all the members, (2) that it is a co-operative unit working for the welfare of each of its members. It is now a well-known fact that where there is lack of affection and disagreement in a family the children suffer, particularly in their ability to be sociable and to become integrated in any wider community.

As the child grows he is able to enter larger groups and identify himself with these. The first is the class in the school which he attends. Later on, at about seven or eight, he begins to be able to recognize the whole school as a unified community of which he himself is an active member. A child's capacity to accept responsibilities towards the community either of class or school, and to accept working for it depends entirely on whether (1) the community works harmoniously as a unit for the welfare of all its members; (2) he, the child, feels himself respected as a member of the community and is allowed to take an active share in some aspects at least of the organization.

The years from eight to eleven see the gradual establishment of strong, fairly closed and stable groups of friends. They are the years of 'secret' societies, pass words, mysterious adventures, badges, secret signs and the beginning of friendly competitions between groups. These do not happen overnight nor is their growth easy and painless. On the contrary, their development needs fairly frequent assistance from the adult world. Because the children are older and more experienced and their intelligence more highly developed than it was in their younger years, the adult help has to be wiser, more sensitive and discreet than before if it is to be acceptable. If the children feel that the grown-ups have put themselves on pedestals and try to wield an unquestioned and unquestionable authority over them, they, the children, will withdraw into their gangs from the grown-up world, withdraw their confidence and place themselves over against the adults, hostile and suspicious. The adults then can no longer help the children in sorting themselves out, adjusting their quarrels, taking both personal and group defeats in games and competitions, in helping the less socialized ones to gain social control and the timid to gain confidence and courage. The adults also lose heavily by this, for the children, by withdrawing from the adult world, fail to become active, social members of the whole community.

Here again the responsibility lies with the adults since it is their task, as the more mature and conscious persons, to prepare and facilitate the children's work of growing progressively into the small child community of the gang,

then the class, then the school and finally the communities
of the outside world.

Children vary very considerably both in their capacities
and need for social companionship and their individual
feelings for and about the group or community. It is one
of the tasks of the adults to bring the group to accept, or
at least tolerate, individual feelings and attitudes in one
member which may not be those of the majority; that is
to say to broaden the outlook and the socially accepted
framework of the community to include individual diver-
gences. Naturally this only applies to attitudes and feelings
which are not anti-social.

The most important aspect of the adult's position is that
of keeping the confidence of the children as they grow out
of babyhood. Now you cannot keep the confidence of the
young and remain an autocrat who is never in the wrong.
As the children have developed they are certain to have
found the Achilles' heel of each one of the adults of their
own small world. If we take the children into our confidence
we thereby admit our own fallibility and are then in a
position to make clear to them that we have, in practice,
more experience and knowledge than they and that by
virtue of these we can help them in their own struggle to
get socially adjusted. The children who have the measure
of the adult's strength and limitations are those who will
benefit most from the adult's help.

Because children turn so much more to group activity
during these last years before puberty the adults can help
them most by providing them with equipment which lends
itself chiefly to group play and not to solitary play or games
for two or three players. For instance, out-of-doors children
want the tools for the team games which they, the children,
organize, such as cricket sets, footballs, tents. The children
should be able and willing to make for themselves a great

many of the things they require. The workshop and studio are rooms which should always be in use at this age. Even in making things children will begin to work in groups after the age of eight or nine and this is just one aspect of their healthy social development.

Chapter Nine

THE PRIMARY SCHOOL'S TASK

THE EFFECT OF THE PRIMARY SCHOOL CURRICULUM

As a people, we are very conscious of the task of the school in 'character development', 'personality growth', 'all-round development' of the child, and so on. We talk about these aspects of growth, we write about them, but when we look at our schools, what evidence have we of these ideas being put into practice? Apart from a few schools, which in fact are the exceptions which prove the rule more than anything else, we see children attending from 9 a.m. to 12 noon and again from 1.30 to 4 p.m., or it may be 9 a.m. to 12.30 and 2 to 4 p.m. During these five and a half hours the children sit at desks, or maybe tables, having lessons. One period may be singing, or music and movement or P.T. in the assembly hall; one period, with any luck, may be given over to dramatic work, painting or handwork. Under no circumstances are the children free to organize their activity themselves either individually or in groups. They have a short break in both morning and afternoon school, of about ten or fifteen minutes. Apart from having some member of the staff patrolling the playground the children are free then. But the shortness of the break, the lack of equipment, and the crowding of the playground which makes it quite impossible for the teacher adequately to supervise what the children are doing, makes it impossible for the children to organize any creative or purposeful activity. Many of the children, particularly if they are timid or shy, dread, rather than welcome, the break, because they are liable to be teased or hurt by other children.

Over all looms the prospect of the 11+ examination hanging like a sword of Damocles over staff and pupils alike. We cannot alter this fact at present, though the tripartite system of education is at last being seriously criticized, but it is all too often used as an excuse for refusing to break with the tradition of the three Rs. It is said that if children spend some time doing other things than practising these skills they will not be up to the standard required in this highly competitive examination. Now no one wishes to reduce any child's chance of what is at present virtually the only suitably academically advanced secondary education and which is only available for 25 per cent of the child population: therefore if failure to spend a great deal of time practising writing, reading and arithmetic really did mean less chance of being sufficiently well educated, we would have to accept the present average primary school curriculum, in favour of preparation for that examination. But in fact this is not so, there is a maximum point of saturation in practising these occupations, beyond which no child can absorb anything more, and many will begin to unlearn if kept too long at the same task. Children learn facts quicker and retain them better if their time-table is more varied and if they occupy themselves in their own way with a variety of materials, including the choice of work at the three Rs, for at least some part of each school day. This is, of course, quite apart from the question of development of other aspects of character than pure intellectual attainments. How do imagination, creativeness, practical skills and the whole gamut of social self-controls fare in the average school curriculum? There is little or no place for them. The argument against their having a place within the school is twofold. One is that the children have sufficient opportunity for 'play' in their out-of-school hours. The other is that they can develop the various kinds of self-control, learn to concentrate, tolerate failure, develop consideration for and tolerance of others, gain courage and show initiative, within the organized framework of class activity and organized games. While this is, to a great extent, possible at secondary school age, it does not happen in early childhood. As has already been pointed out earlier in the book, it seems that young children are only able to develop these characteristics of self-control, social qualities and leadership as well as personal capacity for initiative, concentration and imaginative development, if they are free to develop their own activities and plan and carry out their own group occupations. As for 'play', it is certainly true that children have some time for it between school and bedtime and during their long holidays. But here again, as has been previously pointed out, it is not sufficient just to have playtime without the help and guidance from sympathetic and tactful adults.

THE PLACE OF FREE ACTIVITY IN THE SCHOOL

From the viewpoint of both play and creative art and hand-work activities the school is, by its very essence and organization, the most suitable setting for growing children. The primary school should therefore quite deliberately and consciously provide both the material and time for children to occupy themselves individually and in groups. So long as we continue to have classes of forty

The Primary School's Task

and over in our junior schools it is virtually impossible to do either, except on a very inadequate scale. However, we are becoming conscious, as a nation, of the mockery of real education that such overcrowding creates, so that we shall have, in the not too distant future, to re-think and re-plan the whole of the school system.

When we do this, and do it wisely, the primary school will come into its own. The need for space, for small groupings of children, for garden playgrounds as well as asphalt ones and playing fields, for superised play periods with adequate play materials, will all become as necessary as the present time-table for the 3 Rs, history, geography and nature study.

At present many valiant infant schools struggle to give the children of five and six as much opportunity for such creative, free occupations, under teacher supervision, as their small space, overcrowding and limited play material allows. Very few junior schools do this. Whether the loom of the examination is becoming more threatening because nearer, or whether it is because we think that only infants still require to play, children after seven are expected to devote the five and a half hours of schooling to doing what the teacher tells them to do. Just as the children reach that interesting stage of group consciousness and with it the capacity for group loyalty, we prevent them from developing them within the school. We prevent this by giving the children neither time nor space to organize their own activities within the school. By doing this we give ourselves no opportunity for gaining the children's confidence by helping them in their social development, and we lose thereby any chance we might have of helping them to achieve and strengthen their feeling of belonging to their class or school community, with its responsibilities, loyalties and willingly-accepted communal tasks and duties.

The Primary School's Task

Children cannot feel they really belong to a social group which includes adults and is concerned with the serious tasks of life unless they feel they play an important and responsible part in that organization. We cannot give children this feeling unless we do in fact give them an important part to play. We can, however, only do this, without reducing the school to chaos, by helping the children, from their earliest years in school to organize their own social life, so that they learn to co-operate and help each other in their activities and at the same time showing them at each stage and with each incident in which they require our aid, how the same co-operation and help are required to make the whole social group, be it the small unit of the class or the larger one of the school, function efficiently.

At five or six years the children who have at least one free play period at school as well as handwork and activity periods in which they may work independently or in groups at occupations of their choice, need their teacher just as much as a friendly adviser and helper. The teacher who witnesses her pupils' social play, their squabbles, their reconciliations, their 'sharing' or inability to share, their bids for leadership and power, their tentative advances to each other, and their withdrawals and who, by her qualities of understanding and sympathy, is able to help them in all their problems, struggles and difficulties, will be held in great respect as well as loved. She will be considered both wise and useful as well as knowledgeable and authoritative, so that the children will naturally turn to her for advice.

Since play is still the most important part of life, even in the junior years, the children will show in it their abilities for leadership, initiative, organizing, planning, resourcefulness and so on. Although of course children's capacities very considerably in these characteristics just as much as in others, all children are potential leaders to some degree, just as all have some imagination and initiative. Whether or not they develop these potentialities depends on many factors. The most important of these is the opportunities for very varied play and games which will create leadership of vary varied kinds. One child may be just the leader for a game of fathers and mothers, another for an expedition to the North Pole. One child will show imagination in organizing a play, another in planning a village in the sandpit. Another important factor is the skill and understanding of the teacher who tactfully helps to create situations which enable a less forceful and pushing child to come to the fore. The teacher also helps indirectly by giving confidence and security to those children who need them.

CHILDREN'S IDEAS OF JUSTICE

Children begin to be concerned with questions of 'fairness' round about the age of five, particularly if they have been in a nursery school and had experience of living and playing in groups. The grown-ups so frequently say things such as 'It isn't fair for you to take all the building bricks' or 'It is fair to take turns or to share the sweets out', that the children become conscious of one aspect of their relationship to one another which consists of 'justice'. Naturally at first the fairness is only considered by each child, as his exclusive right; everything is 'fair' whereby he gets what he wants and unfair when he fails to get it.

Many adults who have had to deal with children between five and eleven and who are ceaselessly bombarded with moans of 'It isn't fair, it isn't fair' may heartily wish that the children had never learnt the word or its meaning. A little while ago I met a teacher who, coming from a school in which the children had a great deal of free play, was used to the problems arising from 'it's not fair', had gone to an infant school where neither at school, nor in the streets where the children played did the question of 'fairness' ever arise. To her horror she found that the children of five, six and seven had no idea at all of social behaviour in their mixed games. They fought, threw stones at each other, kicked, bit and bullied without anyone thinking there was anything wrong. Children did not protest at being hurt, but merely cried and ran away, and those who witnessed acts of aggression took them for granted. It would seem that a sense of fairness, the awareness of such a thing as human justice are not inborn, nor even necessarily arise from of their own accord from group play, but must be developed consciously within a social setting.

Each child must, through frequent, and often bitter, experience, learn that fairness must apply to all, and that fairness for one individual may involve sacrifice and restraint on the part of others at that moment. This they can only learn with the help of adults on whom the responsibility falls for seeing that justice is done.

For the younger children in the infant school the help of the adult is required in settling squabbles about toys which are desired by several, about taking turns, sharing equipment, not resorting to blows to settle differences. These are simple problems and usually are settled quickly or else the group play dissolves. Among older children, with whom group play has become more elaborate, with highly developed sets of rules and regulations, obligations, secret vows, 'cross my hands and heart' to prove truthfulness, the demands of the games require far more control, tolerance and respect for others from each member of the group. Their play also requires obedience, courage and resourcefulness from the participants. These characteristics are essential for the well-being of community life in class-

room and school. Children who have had constant help
from their teachers in their group play, when they have
fallen out, in the form of settling difficulties with members
who could not play fair, or accept orders from appointed
leaders, who have deceived, stolen, broken promises and
so on, come easily to recognize the need for the same
characteristics within the communal framework of the
classroom and school life.

Class meetings and school meetings also, when only
juniors are concerned, without infants, are far more effective in instilling social group feelings of responsibility, than
private 'talks' with individual wrong-doers by head
teachers. Children learn much better through discussing
themselves and their behaviour in groups; judgement
passed on anti-social behaviour of one member of the
group after discussion of that behaviour not only has a
deeper and more lasting influence on the child concerned,
but it has an equally good effect on all the children who
are thereby brought to think of the social implications and
consequences of their own behaviour. It also helps children
to learn that hard lesson of accepting criticism that is just
and intended to aid them in their difficulties, without getting angry or annoyed and taking everything as a personal
affront.

In particular the need for honesty and truthfulness are
realized far more acutely by children who are at the 'gang'
stage, because they find in the practice of their more
elaborate games and reliable constant friendships, that
without these qualities neither games nor friendship are
possible. They find from their own experience that liars
cannot be believed, that thieves cannot be trusted, that
cowards cannot be relied upon. They discover the value,
in their personal relationships within their play, not only
of such obvious qualities as truth and honesty, but also

of hard work, resoutcefulness, courage, grit, kindness and generosity. When they have discovered these it is not far to go to apply them to the life of the community, if the teacher helps them to bridge the gap. When they have actually experienced the advantages of these qualities, in however small a degree, they are far more likely to accept their necessity in class life. Personal loyalties grow out of the recognition of such social qualities both in oneself and in others and communal loyalties for class or school or any other social group, also grow out of the concrete expression of such qualities by the members of the group in order to make the communal life and activities better and happier for all. Unless the children do benefit as a group from the expression of their self-control, their capacity for taking responsibilities, for consideration of others, even if the form is no more than verbal praise from the teacher, their communal loyalty will not grow, but recede.

In a small junior school the garden contained many apple and pear trees. In the autumn there were naturally always some children who could not resist the temptation to pick the fruit and eat it. All the fruit was given to the children and they knew this. They were always encouraged to help with the picking and helpers were rewarded with some of the pickings at the end of the work.

One year the number of children who helped themselves to fruit illegally was sufficiently large for the teachers to be seriously concerned about it, and their worry increased when the children failed to control their behaviour after having been reminded and warned of the consequences of such behaviour, and after having suffered the consequences which were to be forbidden the use of the garden for a time and forego their share of fruit when it was served at meal-times. The question of communal property was discussed at a meeting of all the juniors. All the guilty children freely admitted their guilt and some then told the teachers that the grown-ups should not have fruit trees in the garden, so that there should be no temptation to pick, or that a teacher should be watching them all the time they were playing in the garden! When all the children were then asked if they would prefer not to have the fruit, or to be policed during the whole of their play-time they unanimously agreed that they wanted neither of these possibilities. It was pointed out quite clearly that the price of this communal advantage, fruit, was self-control on the part of each member of the community. One very cautious fruit-stealer then solemnly announced: 'I can't promise I won't take any more, because I might break my promise, but I will try not to do it.' In actual fact there was no more fruit stealing that year. Of course social behaviour does not always bring such a tangible and obvious reward, for children find it very difficult indeed to find any benefit in such things as cleanliness or even tidiness, and communal school life could not progress satisfactorily without them. Nevertheless, if the teachers have won the confidence of the children, through their constant willingness to help them over their difficulties, they will be able to make it clear that pleasant communal life requires these qualities. Their help will strengthen the children's intention to try.

CONCLUSION

Children's characteristics are as much a product of the environment in which they have been brought up and the forces they have encountered, as of inheritance. We cannot at present influence inheritance; we do not know what it consists of in any individual, since we cannot test character at birth, and anything we test later in life is a complex product of inheritance and environment. We can control, plan and order the environment and we should do it in such a way as to give a child the maximum opportunity of developing all his abilities to their fullest extent, including his capacity for social communal living and activity. A brilliant boy or girl who cannot play or work within a group, loses potential intellectual advantages as well as social happiness, just as a child who gives up all individual creativeness and individuality in order to be sociable, loses the capacity to develop his own qualities and gifts. Since play is the essence of life in early childhood it is through it that children gain knowledge and understanding as well as their ability to become socialized; it is therefore clearly our duty to provide them with the environment, the material, and the sympathetic adult help and understanding at all stages of early childhood which will make the play rich, purposeful and educational.

Appendix I

THE Nursery School Association of Great Britain, of 1 Park Crescent, W.1, opened a workshop in 1942 to supply play equipment for war nurseries when this came into short supply owing to war-time restrictions. This workshop not only supplies the right kind of play material, but its members conduct training courses in home toy-making for all persons engaged in war-time nursery work.

The most important characteristic of the N.S.A. workshop is that it is staffed by persons who are not only skilled craftsmen and artists, but who know from observation and experience what children need. They have also collected information from teachers and schools. They have carefully and scientifically studied the way in which children play and use their various toys. They consequently know where the chief strain will come on a toy, e.g. that wheels on all pull-and-push-along toys such as trains, trolleys, etc., are the point at which the toy first breaks down. Wheels are therefore put on with the greatest care and greatest reinforcement (screws, washers, very strong axles, etc.). They know, not only the kind of toys which children need at different ages, but they also know down to the smallest detail the necessary characteristics and qualities needed for each separate toy. For example, all carts, prams and trolleys are made big enough and strong enough to carry a small child of pre-school age and their wheels are very well constructed.

The N.S.A. has a large exhibition room with examples of each one of the toys which are made in the workshop; there are detailed instructions with each toy on how to make it, and every toy in the room can be made by anyone who has even the slightest knowledge of how to use hammer, drill and saw, needle and cotton.

Appendix

Anyone who is interested in children's toys and how to make them should certainly visit this exhibition. Certainly, if you want to know, not only what to give a child, but what to look for in the particular toy, go to the N.S.A. Nancy Catford, the director of the workshop, has recently written a book on *Making Nursery Toys*, published by Frederick Muller at 3s. 6d.

All the toys in the illustrations were made in the Nursery School Association workshop.

Appendix II

LIST OF TOYS AND MATERIALS

OUTDOOR EQUIPMENT

Climbing frames	2–6	years
Slide	2–6	,,
Funboat	2–6	,,
Sandpit—cheapest to make at home	2–6	,,
Carts, trucks, wheelbarrows	3–5	,,
Sand toys—home produce cheaper	2–6	,,
Tricycles, kiddicars—any toy shop	3–5	,,
Bicycles—any toy shop	5–6	,,
Bats, balls, reins—any toy shop	2–6	,,
Swing, rings, rope ladders	3–6	,,
Gardening tools—any shop	3–6	,,
Skipping ropes	5–11	,,
Gardening tools—'Romanco'	3–11	,,
Footballs	6–11	,,
Bows and Arrows	8–11	,,
Cricket sets	8–11	,,
Tents	8–11	,,
Rubber pails	2–11	,,

INDOOR EQUIPMENT

For sense training

Hollow building blocks	2–6	years
Small solid building blocks	2–5	,,
'Pull-along' train ⎱ 'Pull-along' barge ⎰	2–4	,,

Tip trucks	2–5	years
Wooden animals on wheels	18 months–3	,,
String of wooden rings and beads	6–12	months
Musical box, solid rattles	6–12	,,
Spoons, wooden blocks	6–12	,,
Balls	6 months–6	years
Trolley filled with wooden cubes	18 ,, –3	,,
Easy puzzles and 'fitting' pictures	2–3	,,
Posting box	1–3	,,
Nest of boxes, bowls and rings	1–3	,,
Enamelled bead wagon	18 months–2	,,
Wooden boats for bath	18 ,, –3	,,
Hammer pegs	18 ,, –3	,,
Pegs and squares	18 ,, –3	,,
Beads on sticks	1 ,, –3	,,
Kiddicraft train builder	3–6	,,

Imaginative Play

Wooden trains, trams, cars, boats, aeroplanes	2–5	years
Dolls and woolly animals—any shop	2–6	,,
Washable dolls and woolly animals	1–6	,,
Doll's furniture and equipment	3–6	,,
Animals, Noah's ark	3–6	,,
Little lead animals and other toys—any shop	3–8	,,
All 'dressing-up' material	3–11	,,
Make-up	6–11	,,
Large supply of 'oddments', particularly in way of old blankets, pots and pans, wooden boxes etc.		

Constructional Toys

Kiddicraft interlocking bricks	4–6	years
Kiddicraft rubber bricks	6 months–2	,,
Matador—only from Abbatt's	5–8	,,
Pick-a-brick	5–8	,,
Weekin screw toys	3–6	,,
Makimore	4–6	,,
Lott's bricks	5–8	,,
Lott's Tudor bricks	5–8	,,
Minibricks	4–11	,,
Bayko	5–11	,,
Multibuilder	4–6	,,

Appendix

Connector	5–10 years
Brickplayer	8–11 ,,
Trix	7–11 ,,
Meccano	8–11 ,,
Dinky builder	8–11 ,,
Escor constructional toys . . .	4–7 ,,

Everyday skills

Brooms, brushes, pans, washing equipment, etc.	2–5 years
Paper, pencils, paints, brushes . . .	2–6 ,,
Scissors, paste, coloured paper, thin cardboard .	3–6 ,,
Large box for all remnants, oddments, etc.	
Carpentry tools	4–11 ,,
Simple weaving frames	5–11 ,,
Large knitting needles	6–11 ,,
Wool canvas, wools and needles . .	4–11 ,,
Finer embroidery needles, canvas and cotton .	8–11 ,,

Material for the 3 R's

Wooden clock face	5–6 years
Wooden cut-out letters and numbers . .	4–6 ,,
Cut-out picture and model makers	
(Many French ones published by Flammarion, Album du Pere Castor, are excellent.)	
Self-teaching letter and picture matching . .	4–6 ,,
Self-teaching number puzzles . . .	4–6 ,,

Games

Card games recommended:

Laundry line out	7–11 years
Counties of England	9–11 ,,
Flying Hats	8–11 ,,
Touring England	9–11 ,,
Contact Quiz	10–11 ,,
Picture Lotto	7–11 ,,
Peter Rabbit Race	7–11 ,,
Draughts	8–11 ,,
Chess	8–11 ,,
Dominoes	5–8 ,,

Appendix

Music

Drums, bells, cymbals, triangles . . .	3–6	years
Musical boxes (wooden ones with lids and glass tops)	15 months–6	,,
Gramophone	3–11	,,

Books

Cousland, *My Little London* . . .	5–6	,,
The Farm Gate	2–4	,,
My Alphabet	3–4	,,
'Little Golden Books'	2–4	,,
Flack, *Angus* books	3–4	,,
Bannerman, *Little Black Sambo* series .	4–6	,,
Buckles, *Three Little Ducklings* . .	4–5	,,
De Brunhoff, *Babar* books . . .	3–6	,,
Gag, *Millions of Cats* . . .	4–6	,,
Snippy and Snappy . . .	4–6	,,
V. L. Burton, *Katy and the Big Snow* . .	2–4	,,
Diana Ross, The *Little Red Engine* books .	4–6	,,
G. James, The *John and Mary* series . .	5–8	,,
Stephen Bone, *The Little Boy and His House* .	6–8	,,
The Little Boy and His Ship . .	6–8	,,
J. L. Brisley, *Milly-Molly-Mandy* books .	7–9	,,
G. Greene, The *Little Fire Engine* books .	4–6	,,
Garrick, *Picture Tales from the Russian* .	6–9	,,
Ardizzone, Various books . . .	6–8	,,
Derrick, *The Ark* book . . .	4–6	,,
C. Webb, *Butterwick Farm* . . .		
The North Pole before Lunch . .		
The Story of Noah . . .	5–7	,,
Jungle Picnic		
L. L. Brooke, *Johnnie Crow's Garden* . .	4–5	,,
O. Bowen, *Taddy Tadpole* . . .	6	,,
Flack, *The Story about Ping* . . .	7	,,
Bone, *The Book of Splendid Planes* . .	4–6	,,
Hosking, *Friends at the Zoo* . . .	5–6	,,
Borlanger, *Infants of the Zoo* . . .	5–6	,,
Lisa, *The Magic Collar* . . .	6	,,
Lois Lenski		
The Baby Car	3–5	,,
Baby Ann		

Appendix

Nancy Catford, *Animal* series	3–5	years
B. Haden, *Whiffy McMann*	2–6	,,
Thornton Burgess, *Animal Stories* series	7–9	,,
Petersham, *The Ark of Father Noah*	4–6	,,
Dent's *Everyday* series		
Flack, *Liang Lo*	6	,,
Great Bullfrog	6	,,
Flammarion, *Bonjour et Bonsoir*	2–3	,,
Hale, *Orlando* books	6–8	,,
Flack, *William and his Kitten*		
What to do about Molly		
Polly and Jane	6–8	,,
Helen and Margaret Bynion, *A Day at the Seaside*	4–6	,,
'Bantam Books'		
Ashley, *John and Mary's Shopping Day*	4–6	,,
John and Mary's Spring Cleaning		
A. Utley, *Little Grey Rabbit* series	6–8	,,
Beatrix Potter, *Peter Rabbit* series	5–7	,,
G. Heward, *Ameliaranne* series	6–8	,,
G. Rae, *Mary Plain* series	7–10	,,
B. E. Codd, *Worzel Gummidge*	8–10	,,
A. A. Milne, *Winnie the Pooh*	8–10	,,
House at Pooh Corner	8–10	,,
C. S. Lewis, *The Lion, the Witch and the Wardrobe*	8–10	,,
B. Nicholls, *The Stream that Stood Still*	7–9	,,
H. Lofting, *Doctor Doolittle* series	7–9	,,
L. Carrol, *Alice's Adventures in Wonderland*	8–10	,,
R. Kipling, *The Just-So Stories*	7–10	,,
The Jungle Book	8–10	,,
P. L. Travers, *Mary Poppins*	9–10	,,
M. Norton, *The Magic Bed-Knob*	8–9	,,
K. Graham, *The Wind in the Willows*	10–11	,,
F. Nesbitt, *The Treasure Seekers*, etc.	10–11	,,
K. Barne, *Dusty's Windmill*	10–11	,,
F. Garnett, *The Family from One End Street*	10–11	,,
A. Ransome, *Swallows and Amazons* etc	9–11	,,
N. Streatfield, *The Fearless Treasure*	10–11	,,
G. Trease, *Bows Against the Barons* etc	10–11	,,
J. Spyri, *Heidi* etc.	10–11	,,
Various *Puffin* books		

Appendix

Marjory Flack, *Angus* books
'Leila Berg books'
'Francoise books', *Jeanne, Marie and Patapon*
Alf Proysen, *Mrs. Pepperpot*
Astrid Lingren, *Pippi Longstocking*
M. Bond, *Paddington Bear*
'Ladybird Books'
There are many excellent information books for children on all scientific, historical and geographical topics.

Poetry and Songs
W. de la Mare, *This Year–Next Year*
    Fairies in Plenty
E. Farjeon, *Over the Garden Wall*
Fyleman, *Here we Come a-Piping*
    Old Nursery Rhymes (illustrated)
Sheed & Ward's, *A First Poetry Book*
A. A. Milne, *When We Were Very Young*
    Now We Are Six
Clarendon Song Book, 60 *Songs for Little Children*
Augener, *Sing-Song from Sweden. I.*
R. L. Stevenson, *A Child's Garden of Verses*
A Puffin Quartet of Poets, edited by Eleanor Graham
John Clare, *The Wood is Sweet*
Fairings in Plenty, edited by Basil Blackwell
For your Delight, edited by Ethel Fowler
Modern Verse for Little Children, edited by Michael Williams
Paths to Parnassus book 2, Gossamer and Thistledown,
    edited by T. D. Campbell
Pedlar's Pack Bk. 1, edited by A. Newell, A. & C.
    Black Ltd.